TUG OF WAR

TUG OF WAR

TODAY'S GLOBAL CURRENCY CRISIS

PAUL ERDMAN

St. Martin's Press
New York

ISBN 0-312-15899-8

Library of Congress Cataloging-in-Publication Data

Erdman, Paul Emil, 1932-
　　Tug of war : today's global currency crisis / Paul Erdman.
　　　　p.　cm.
　　Includes bibliographical references and index.
　　ISBN 0-312-15899-8
　　1. Foreign exchange. 2. Foreign exchange administration.
I. Title.
HG3851.E673 1996
332.45—dc20　　　　　　　　　　　　　　　　96-19401
　　　　　　　　　　　　　　　　　　　　　　　　CIP

Book Design: Acme Art, Inc.

First Edition: September 1996
10 9 8 7 6 5 4 3 2 1

CONTENTS

LIST OF FIGURES AND TABLES

Figures

Tables

TUG OF WAR

Part I

1. Introduction

THE CURRENCY MARKET TODAY plays a role in almost everybody's life. We realize that as we increasingly travel abroad. When you go to London these days and change your dollars into pounds, you don't get nearly as many pounds as you used to. Because of the very unfavorable exchange rate you have to pay the equivalent of five dollars for a lousy cup of coffee. You have just learned that dramatic changes in the international value of your currency—in this case, the dollar—can really hurt.

Porsche found out the same thing. Its cars are made in Stuttgart, Germany, and so its costs are in deutsche marks (DM). Years ago, when the DM was at over three to the dollar, a Porsche that cost 100,000 DM to make in Germany could be sold for $38,000 in the United States, leaving Porsche with a nice profit. By 1995, with the DM at 1.40 to the dollar, Porsches costing 100,000 DM had to be priced at over $75,000 in the United States. The result: Americans stopped buying Porsches, and the German company almost went broke.

Currency fluctuations also have a major effect on investing, which today is an international game. Many American mutual funds and pension funds have gone global. Those that invested in the Swiss stock market in 1995 did very well: Not only did Swiss shares go up in value but so did the Swiss franc relative to the dollar, meaning investors got an enhanced return. (In dollar terms, the only stock market that outperformed the American market in 1995 was Switzerland's.) By contrast, the Mexican peso and the stock market in Mexico City tanked in 1995, with the result that Americans who had invested in Mexican stocks saw their dollar value sink by 50 percent.

What is of overriding importance, however, is what currency fluctuations, and especially currency crises, can do to a nation's economy. A classic example of this occurred in 1995, when the yen soared to 79 to the dollar, four times higher than it was just 25 years ago, while the dollar plunged. This meant that Japan's entire export industry—the engine that drives the Japanese economy—was in danger of being priced out of world markets. As a result, Japan sank ever deeper into recession, while the stock exchange in Tokyo hit new lows. But with the dollar now much lower in terms of not only the yen but also all major currencies, products made in America were more competitive in world markets than they had been for many years. Exports boomed, America's economy flourished, and the stock market in New York soared to the highest level in history.

So currency movements cut both ways. In fact, they have become a central factor in the economic tug of war between nations. This is especially true of the rivalry between the world's two economic superpowers, the United States and Japan. It was their currencies—the dollar and the yen—that were at the center of the currency instability that began in 1995 and continues today.

TODAY'S CURRENCY CRISIS

A number of questions now arise about this currency instability. What happened to bring it to a head in 1995? Which currency was and still is in crisis, the yen or the dollar? And who is to blame, the Americans or the Japanese?

If you ask these questions in Washington, you'll get answers like these:

- The blame rests squarely on past Japanese mercantilistic trade policies fostered by the Ministry of International Trade and Industry (MITI) and an intransigent Japanese bureaucracy.

- These policies inevitably led to monstrous trade surpluses with the rest of the world in general and with the United States in particular.
- As these surpluses kept growing and accumulating, the inevitable result was a global shortage of yen, just like there was a global shortage of dollars after World War II (known then as "the dollar gap") when the United States ran huge trade surpluses with a war-ravaged world.
- When any commodity or currency is in short supply, its price goes up, a process that often ends in a "buying climax."
- At the beginning of 1995 that "buying climax" occurred in the world's currency markets, leading to a Yen crisis where it was valued at under 80 to the dollar as compared to 360 yen to the dollar not that long ago.

If you ask these same questions in Tokyo, the answer will probably be quite different. From the Japanese point of view,

- The blame rests squarely on the reckless fiscal policies of the United States government, which has been running huge budget deficits for decades.
- These policies led to a quadrupling of America's national debt, from under $1 trillion when Ronald Reagan became president to $5 trillion today. Such fiscal follies inevitably led to huge and rising trade deficits, especially with the highly efficient and thus highly competitive Japan. As a result of these deficits, the world was flooded with dollars.
- When any commodity or currency is in surplus, its price goes down, a process that often culminates in a "selling climax." That selling climax, promoted by a new breed of extremely powerful currency speculators, occurred in early 1995, resulting in a dollar crisis

that pushed its value down to 79 yen and 1.34 DM. The dollar has recovered somewhat in the meantime, but the basic problem has by no means been resolved.

Which answer is right? Was it a yen crisis or a dollar crisis? And what comes next? Will the global dollar glut continue to grow in the years ahead? Will foreigners—who now own 1.3 *trillion* dollars worth of American assets—be willing to continue to hold them? Or will they decide to cut their losses if the dollar starts to weaken further and start the dollar-dumping process all over again?

If so, then the 1995 currency crisis will have been the mere prelude to a dollar meltdown that could leave the international currency system in total disarray, resulting in the irreversible decline and fall of the dollar as the world's reserve currency. The dollar would be gradually replaced by a basket of currencies made up of yen, Swiss francs and deutsche marks (to be replaced eventually by the Euro) as the central banks of the world began to seriously diversify their portfolios. Because these hard currencies would be bought in huge quantities, however, their value relative to the dollar would continue to increase. As a result, the export industries of Japan, Germany, and Switzerland would find it increasingly difficult to survive if they continued to serve foreign markets from domestic production bases. As they shifted more and more of their output to factories based abroad, domestic output would sink, and unemployment would rise to levels not seen in these countries since World War II. The next currency crisis, then, would be replaced by a full-blown global economic crisis.

The last domino to fall, paradoxically, would be the economy of the United States. In the beginning, American exports, priced in terms of the cheapest dollar ever seen in the twentieth century, would soar, and the American stock market would do the same. But ultimately the falling dollar would catch up with both of them. As has happened in other countries, massive devaluation would result in the return of inflation as the cost of imported goods soared, setting off an upward spiralling of all prices. The Federal Reserve would then have no choice but to step in and drastically raise short-term interest rates. At that point, though, even higher rates would no longer be sufficient to entice investors to stay in dollar assets. As they began to dump U.S. Treasury notes and bonds, bond prices would plummet and long-term interest rates would skyrocket. The only remaining buyer of last resort of dollars would be the U.S. Treasury and the American central bank, the Federal Reserve. In order to buy in dollars by the tens of billions, they would have to borrow massive amounts of yen, marks, and francs through swap agreements with other central banks, the IMF, and the Bank for International Settlements. But it would be too late. The damage would already have been done, and it would spill over into the stock market. The American financial bubble would burst.

How likely is this worst case scenario? Is there a more likely "happy ending"? Let's look at both possibilities by beginning with the immediate origins of the currency crisis of 1995. It started in an unlikely place with a currency that few people paid much attention to: the Mexican peso.

2

MEXICO WAS AN UNLIKELY PLACE for the currency crisis to begin because in recent years the peso had been a remarkably stable currency.

The stability of the peso was the result of what was considered by the world to be a very "enlightened" policy followed by the Mexican government under the leadership of Harvard graduate President Carlos Salinas de Gortari and his closely knit group of Ivy League–educated financial advisors. They, in essence, tied the peso to the dollar, maintaining the rate of exchange within a very narrow trading band, the lower limit of which was allowed to decline from 3 pesos to the dollar at the beginning of the Salinas regime to 3.5 pesos to the dollar in December of 1994. By buying pesos with dollars when the peso sank too much and selling pesos for dollars when the peso rose too much, the Mexican government could compensate for domestic inflation and maintain the peso's purchasing power parity with the dollar. Such adjustments were engineered in a controlled, steady, predictable manner. This manipulation of the peso (which, in essence, disguised the fact that a stable peso/dollar exchange rate was no longer compatible with Mexico's rising inflation), combined with high domestic interest rates, made Mexico appear to be a very attractive place to invest.

So beginning in 1991, foreign investors—predominantly American institutional investors—attracted by Mexican notes and bonds paying 15 percent and a stock market that was greatly "undervalued" by international standards (with price/earnings ratios substantially below what they were in the United States)—began buying Mexican securities on an unprecedented scale. By the end of 1993, tens of billions of dollars had poured into Mexico City from New York.

In 1994, though, the picture changed. All was no longer well in Mexico. A peasant insurgency had begun in the southern Mexican state of Chiapas, and the front-running presidential candidate handpicked by the PRI ruling party, Donaldo Luis Colosio, was assassinated. Inevitably, investors started to get nervous; the more farsighted among them started to pull their money out of Mexico. Mexican foreign exchange reserves, which at the beginning of the year had totalled $30 billion, fell to $18 billion after the Colosio assassination.

After this initial panic, however, the situation appeared to have stabilized. The presidential elections were carried out in a relatively orderly fashion despite the assassination of José Francisco Ruiz Massien, the former brother-in-law of President Salinas. When the new president, Ernesto Zedillo, and his team moved in to take charge in December 1994, the peso/dollar exchange rate remained steady at 3.5.

But on December 19, like a bolt of lightning out of the blue sky, Zedillo's new government announced that it was going to lower the guaranteed level at which pesos could be exchanged for dollars. This was being done to correct the overvaluation of the peso during the Salinas era during which Mexican prices had risen much faster than they had been compensated for by exchange rate adjustments. On that day 100 pesos would now be worth only $25 instead of the $29 they were worth the day before. This abrupt change in government policy immediately triggered a flight from the peso that was joined en masse as foreigners and Mexicans alike began to seek safer havens abroad for their money. By December 21, just two days later, Mexico's foreign exchange reserves had fallen to $6 billion; on December 22 the Mexican government had no choice but to abandon all efforts to stabilize its currency. It stopped intervening in the foreign exchange market, and announced that the peso would be allowed to float freely in the currency markets, its value to be determined by private sector supply and demand and not by government manipulation. The peso plummeted to 5 to the dollar (meaning that those 100 pesos would now fetch only $20). Although the rate appeared to have temporarily stabilized in early 1995, what had happened had left the New York investment community dazed and confused. They had bet many billions of American investors' dollars on Mexico's future—and now they had been doubled—crossed by the Mexican government.

What had gone wrong? And why had nobody—*nobody*—foreseen this peso devaluation?

The shock in the United States was all the greater because just a year earlier, the United States, Canada, and Mexico had signed an historic agreement that, for the first time, tied their economic destinies together. Under the conditions of the North American Free Trade Agreement (NAFTA) all three countries were now obligated to eliminate all barriers to trade among them. The man who originally championed this idea was the president of Mexico, Carlos Salinas de Gortari. His chief convert to this process in 1992 was Bill Clinton, who that November would become the new president of the United States. The Texas billionaire Ross Perot, another candidate for president, vehemently opposed the concept, and made NAFTA a major political issue of the campaign. If NAFTA became reality, Perot said, it would result in "a great sucking sound" as jobs were sucked out of high-cost United States into low-cost Mexico.

Perot lost. Clinton won. And one year later, before the world's television cameras, a triumphant Carlos Salinas shook hands with a smiling Bill Clinton after they had just signed the NAFTA treaty. Both, in a way, had staked at least part of their political fortunes on its success. Both had to now convince their people that they had done the right thing.

Subsequent events seemingly proved both Clinton and Salinas right. NAFTA appeared to be a win-win situation. As far as Clinton was concerned, contrary to the dire prediction of Ross Perot, American exports to Mexico increased dramatically. For the first time the American Big Three automobile manufacturers were selling cars and vans that had been manufactured in Detroit in the Mexican market. Apple computers were being snapped up by eager buyers in Monterrey and Mexico City. Wal-Mart, the huge and highly successful American retailer, opened American-style superstores throughout Mexico with great success.

Up to this time, Mexicans had always viewed their neighbor to the north with great suspicion. The saying "So far from God, so near to the United States" summed up the prevailing attitude. Now, it seemed, they not only loved everything American but also intended to buy everything American, and the Salinas government did nothing to rein in this process. In fact, in order to allow this buying binge to continue, the Mexican government initiated an extremely dangerous borrowing practice: Even though Mexico increasingly lacked the means to repay them, it began issuing very short-term notes denominated in pesos but with a guaranteed dollar exchange value, called *tesabonos*. The dollars that the issue of these notes brought in were then used to pay for the ever rising importation of American-made consumer goods. This meant that, despite these new loans to Mexico, dollars were still going out faster than they were coming in. It was when the world became aware of the amount of *tesabonos* that the Mexican government had issued that the second stage of the Mexican financial crisis began.

The arithmetic was quite simple. During the month of January 1995, Mexico's foreign exchange reserves had dwindled to just $2 billion dollars. But the amount of *tesabonos* outstanding was now $30 billion. During the first week in February over $1 billion of those notes were coming due. The rest would come due shortly thereafter. Mexico, then, was on the brink of insolvency.

Still worse, the so-called tequila effect had begun working its way south through all of Latin America. As a result of what was happening in Mexico, even Argentina and Brazil, two countries that were in better economic shape than they had been in many a decade, became suspect in the eyes of international investors. Ironically, this erosion of investor confidence occurred barely a month after the leaders of every nation in the Western

Hemisphere, except Fidel Castro, had come to Miami to hear President Clinton proclaim his backing of a Western Hemisphere Common Market stretching from Argentina to Canada. Clinton pledged that it would become a reality early in the twenty-first century.

So it was not just Mexico's destiny that was tied to that of the United States. America had now assumed the mantle of responsibility for all of Latin America. The possibility of Mexican insolvency in this second stage of the peso crisis thus evoked the fear of a domino reaction. If Mexico was allowed to go over the brink into insolvency and default on its foreign debt, the world would inevitably believe that Brazil and Argentina could not be far behind, possibly creating a self-fulfilling prophecy. All of Latin America had become dependent upon foreign investment in the 1990s. Between 1991 and 1994 a total of over $45 billion had been poured into their economies from abroad. If much of that was now yanked out because of a loss of confidence in Latin America, then the entire hemisphere would be in crisis.

President Clinton had no choice but to intervene. His first proposal was for a unilateral $40 billion American bailout. When it became apparent that approval from Congress would not be forthcoming, Clinton decided to go it alone. He, as president, controlled an obscure fund, called the "Exchange Stabilization Fund," that had been created in 1936 at the time of the massive dollar devaluation that took place that year. Its original funding came from the windfall profit that the U.S. Treasury had made on its holdings of gold bullion when the official price of gold was raised from $20.67 to $35 an ounce. By 1995, it had grown to $36 billion. But Clinton soon realized that it would hardly be prudent to commit all of it. After all, the fund was designed to stabilize the international value of the dollar in times of crisis, not that of the peso.

So the Clinton team, led by Secretary of the Treasury Robert Rubin and Deputy Secretary Lawrence Summers, changed tactics. They decided to put together a multilateral

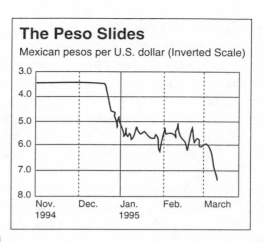

The Peso Slides

Mexican pesos per U.S. dollar (Inverted Scale)

| | Nov. 1994 | Dec. | Jan. 1995 | Feb. | March |

Figure 2.1

rescue package for Mexico; within days they had succeeded. The United States would put up $20 billion from the Exchange Stabilization Fund. A further $32 billion would be added chiefly by the International Monetary Fund (IMF) and the Bank for International Settlements (BIS).

By the end of the first week in February the bailout package was a done deal. The immediate threat of Mexican insolvency was over, but doubts about the future remained. An analyst at the New York investment bank Goldman Sachs said at the time that the recent events might have solved one half of the problem, the financing of the *tesabonos,* but not the other half, the credibility of Mexican institutions. The fall in the value of the peso from late February to mid-March (from 5 to 7.5 to the dollar) proved him right.

Unfortunately for the United States, despite the temporary success of the Mexican bailout, the credibility of another Western Hemisphere country and its currency now began to be seriously questioned. This time it was Canada, America's neighbor to the north and its other new partner within NAFTA, which had come under scrutiny (and not without good reason).

14 |

Canada had become the Western Hemisphere's equivalent of Sweden—a welfare state par excellence where the public sector controlled over half of the economy. The results of the policy of taking care of people from the cradle to the grave—as well-intentioned as it may be—have been the same in both countries: incentives to work gradually disappeared, breeding macroeconomic inefficiencies. This, in turn, resulted in a situation in which public sector costs kept growing, but the economic base could no longer support them, leading to ever larger budgetary deficits, greater and greater government borrowing, and a huge national debt.

In Sweden the economy hit the wall in the early 1990s and sank into a deep and long recession, with unemployment rising to unprecedented levels. In Canada, the national debt soared even higher than Sweden's. This meant that by 1995 almost 50 percent of every dollar spent by the Canadian government had to go to interest payments. To further compound the problem, 40 percent of that national debt was coming due by 1996. The problem was compounded still further by the fact that the Canadian government's borrowings were not restricted to domestic capital markets. As its debt mounted, Canada had increasingly been forced to raise the needed funds abroad. The old saying that the size of the national debt really doesn't matter since "we owe it to ourselves" no longer applied. By early 1995, one-third of Canada's huge national debt was in foreign hands. Where Canada was concerned, "foreign" meant mostly American. This all came to light in early February 1995, when the voice of American capitalism, the *Wall Street Journal,* ran an editorial comparing the Canadian situation with that of Mexico. Overnight everything in Canadian dollars became suspect, from bonds to stocks to bank CDs.

At this point some members of the international financial community took all of this to its logical conclusion. If Canada now went the way of Mexico, the United States would have absolutely no other choice but to bail it out as well. If Mexico had cost America $20 billion, how much would Canada cost? And if Canada went, how far behind could Brazil and Argentina be? And what would their bailouts cost the United States?

Furthermore, could the United States afford all this? Where would it get the money? By borrowing still more from Peter, that is, Japan, in order to bail out Paul (the entire Western Hemisphere)? What would be the consequences of such a move? After all, it was excessive national debt that brought down the Mexican peso and almost brought down the Canadian dollar. And even before all this had started, who was by far and away the world's largest debtor?

The United States of America.

3

HOW HAD THE UNITED STATES GOTTEN INTO SUCH A FIX? There can be little doubt that the currency crisis had its origins in the two-term presidency of Ronald Reagan. It was during those eight years that America's national debt tripled, rising from under $1 trillion before he assumed the presidency to well over $3 trillion when he left. By running huge budgetary deficits even during times of high prosperity, Ronald Reagan accumulated far more national debt than all of his predecessors, starting with George Washington, combined. This process of debt accumulation continued under both his successors until by February 1995 the grand total was $4.5 trillion dollars.

But the problem was not just that the federal government was constantly running budgetary deficits of hundreds of billions of dollars each year. In 13 successive years the nation had also been running international trade deficits, which by the mid-1990s exceeded $150 billion. Foreigners, therefore, had been accumulating ever larger dollar holdings, which were then invested back in the United States. (By definition, current account deficits are matched, dollar for dollar, by capital inflows.) For years this recycling process worked very well. The Japanese, who had the world's largest trade surplus, were the biggest accumulators of dollars and thus the biggest exporters of capital to the world. Much of this capital was going to the United States. The pie charts on page 19 sum up what was happening.

Japanese private investments in the United States were concentrated in three areas—commercial real estate, stocks, and bonds—as well as in major direct investments, such as Mitsubishi's purchase of the Bank of California, or the purchase

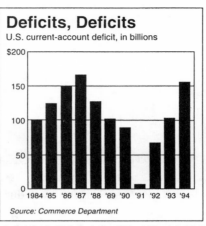

Deficits, Deficits

U.S. current-account deficit, in billions

Source: Commerce Department

Figure 3.1 Source: Bob Davis, "U.S. Trade Gap Widened Again in '94, Making 13 Straight Years of Deficits," *The Wall Street Journal*, March 15, 1995, pp. A2+. Reprinted by permission of *The Wall Street Journal*, © 1995 Dow Jones & Company, Inc. All Rights Reserved Worldwide.

of the Hollywood studio MCA by Matsushita. None of these worked out as expected.

Let's look at Matsushita first. In December 1990, it paid $6.1 billion for MCA. In 1995 it sold 80 percent of its stake in the studio to Seagrams, a Canadian company, for $5.7 billion. So on the surface it appears to have eked out a small profit. But when Matsushita repatriated the cash it received on the sale, it was forced to realize a foreign exchange loss of $1.9 billion (¥ 165 billion).

The Bank of California deal fared no better. Mitsubishi Bank bought the bank in 1984 for $800 million. At that time, the rate of exchange was approximately 250 yen to the dollar. After it bought the bank, Mitsubishi found out that it had to write off huge sums of money stemming from bad loans, most of which involved California real estate. It had no choice but to cover the losses by putting in an additional half billion dollars, for a total investment of $1.3 billion. By 1995, with the exchange rate below 100 yen to the dollar, Mitsubishi had a paper loss in book value equal to well over half of its original investment.

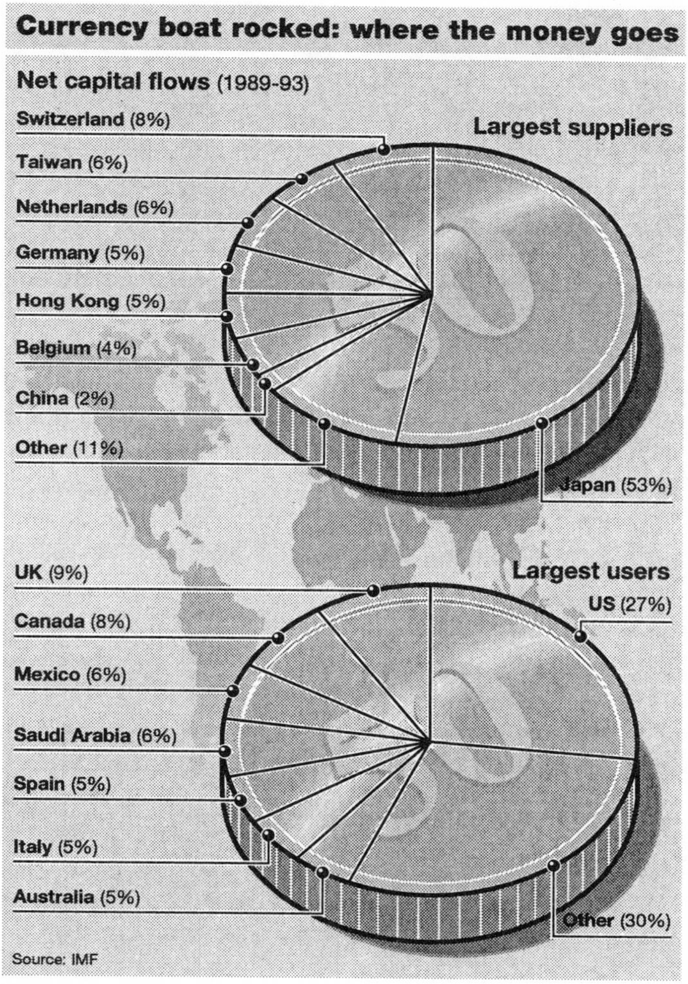

Currency boat rocked: where the money goes

Net capital flows (1989-93)

Largest suppliers

- Switzerland (8%)
- Taiwan (6%)
- Netherlands (6%)
- Germany (5%)
- Hong Kong (5%)
- Belgium (4%)
- China (2%)
- Other (11%)
- Japan (53%)

Largest users

- UK (9%)
- Canada (8%)
- Mexico (6%)
- Saudi Arabia (6%)
- Spain (5%)
- Italy (5%)
- Australia (5%)
- US (27%)
- Other (30%)

Source: IMF

Figure 3.2   Source: Peter Norman, "The Few and the Many," *The Financial Times,* April 28, 1995, p. 16. Reprinted by permission of *The Financial Times* © 1995. All Rights Reserved Worldwide.

| 1 9

But the Japanese losses in the area of direct investment pale when compared to those suffered in other types of investment.

COMMERCIAL REAL ESTATE

During the second half of the 1980s, Japanese investors poured tens of billions of dollars into American commercial real estate, concentrating on such areas as Hawaii, California and New York. Just as the amount of the investments was reaching its peak, however, the United States began experiencing a recession. Commercial real estate prices fell by 20 to 25 percent on average; the value of some types of investments plummeted even further. As the collateral worth of these investments sank, the Japanese banks that had financed the deals were forced to begin calling in their loans. This resulted in the forced sale of many of these properties at huge losses.

Pebble Beach was one such property. In 1990, a Japanese group bought the world-famous golf resort for $880 million. A very high percentage of the financing came from bank loans. The investor soon found out that cash flow from the property fell well below interest costs. When it was forced to sell less than two years later, it got only $500 million back.

Rockefeller Center is another example. In 1989, at the top of the market, Mitsubishi Real Estate accumulated 80 percent of the company that owned the New York landmark for $1.4 billion. At that time the dollar was worth about 150 yen. As with Pebble Beach, when this purchase was revealed an enormous public outcry arose: How could America sit by while the Japanese were taking over these American landmarks? In both cases, that outcry was misdirected. Unfortunately, Mitsubishi had also acquired the $1.3 billion mortgage that had been outstanding against Rockefeller Center. As a glut of office space developed in New York, Mitsubishi soon found out that its mortgage payments far exceeded its rental income. As a result, by

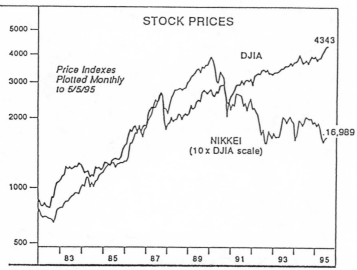

Figure 3.3 Source: *Wright Investor's Newsletter,* Summer 1995. Reprinted by permission of Wright Investor's Service.

1995 Rockefeller Center had already consumed more than $500 million of its owner's cash; with the change in yen/dollar exchange rate, the loss was $1 billion. On May 12, 1995, Mitsubishi Real Estate had no choice but to declare bankruptcy.

These are just two high profile examples of what has happened to Japanese investors in American real estate. How much their real estate losses have been in aggregate is uncertain, but industry experts say they have undoubtedly run into many tens of billions of dollars.

STOCKS

When you look at the performance of the New York Stock Exchange in the 1990s as compared to the Tokyo Stock Exchange, it appears that at least some Japanese investors who put their money in the United States must have fared very well.

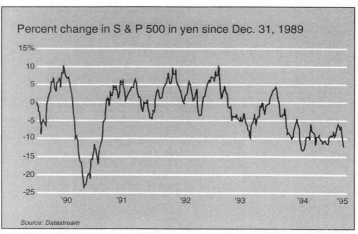

Percent change in S & P 500 in yen since Dec. 31, 1989

Source: Datastream

Figure 3.4 Source: Floyd Norris, "Looking at U.S. Markets Through Japanese Wallets, *The New York Times,* March 12, 1995, p. 15. Reprinted by permission of The New York Times Company, © 1995. All Rights Reserved Worldwide.

Figure 3.3, which traces the Dow Jones Industrial Average (the index based on the stock prices of 30 blue-chip American companies) relative to the Nikkei 225 (the index based on the stock prices of Japan's 225 leading corporations), seems to lead to this conclusion.

But this picture is highly deceiving.

There can be little doubt that investors in Japanese stocks have lost an immense amount of money between the beginning of 1990 and early 1995, during which time the Nikkei 225 plunged from near 40,000 to well under 20,000, meaning that Japanese investors who stayed at home lost over half their money. The Nikkei has recovered to over 20,000 since. Over the same period of time, the American stock market moved in the opposite direction. The broad measure of stock prices, the Standard and Poor's 500, increased 35 percent between 1990 and the beginning of 1995. So the Japanese investor who shifted his money from Tokyo to New York in 1990 must have done very well, right?

Wrong. Despite the fact that American stock prices had been reaching all-time highs, Japanese investors in these stocks

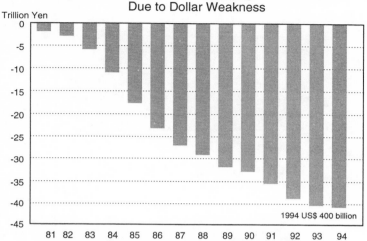

Japan's Cumulative Exchange Rate Loss*
Due to Dollar Weakness

Trillion Yen

1994 US$ 400 billion

81 82 83 84 85 86 87 88 89 90 91 92 93 94

* Cumulative exchange rate loss is Japan's cumulative current account balance using historic
exchange rates minus cumulative current account balance at JPY/USD 100 exchange rate.
Source: Merrill Lynch International Economics.

Figure 3.5 Source: Merrill Lynch Global Economics and Currencies, February 8, 1995.
Reprinted by permission. Copyright © Merrill Lynch, Pierce, Fenner & Smith Incorporated.

"managed" to consistently lose money on their investments. Again, the fault lies with the 41 percent depreciation of the dollar. Add the rise in price of U.S. stocks to the decline of the dollar, and you come to the realization that between mid-1990 and mid-1995 Japanese investors in U.S. equities lost 23 percent of their initial investments.

BONDS, NOTES, LOANS

This is where Japanese investors had their largest losses during the early 1990s. It seemed like the more they lent to the United States (in other words, the more dollar-denominated notes and bonds they bought), the more they lost. This process had been going on, unabated, for two decades. Although it is hard to calculate the total amount the Japanese have lost over time as a | 2 3

Rising Interest Rates; Falling Bond Rates

Interest Fed Funds (NY Fed)

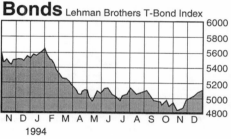

Bonds Lehman Brothers T-Bond Index

Figure 3.6

result of purchases of U.S. fixed income securities and bank loans, Merrill Lynch, an American investment bank, recently estimated that Japan's cumulative current account surpluses totalled approximately $900 billion between early 1980 and 1994. Based on this book value, the currency losses on all overseas Japanese loans and investments had totalled $400 billion. In other words, the difference between what they *paid* for the $900 billion, at the historic exchange rates, and what those dollars were *worth* in 1995, at the now much lower dollar/yen exchange rate, was $400 billion.

But in 1994, like everybody else who had invested in fixed interest securities, the Japanese also started to lose immense amounts of money on the bonds themselves as their prices collapsed. The reason for this was an abrupt change in

The Fate of the Dollar

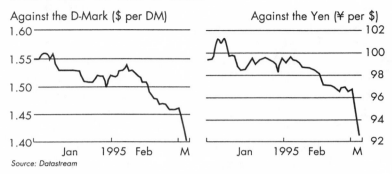

Against the D-Mark ($ per DM)   Against the Yen (¥ per $)

Source: Datastream

Figure 3.7 Source: *The Wall Street Journal,* April/May 1995 Reprinted by permission of *The Wall Street Journal,* © 1995 Dow Jones & Company, Inc. All Rights Reserved Worldwide.

American monetary policy in February of that year. The American economic recovery, which had begun 18 months earlier, had suddenly turned into a boom. American GDP was growing at a rate of over 7 percent. This growth spurt led Alan Greenspan, the Chairman of the Federal Reserve, to believe that things were already beginning to heat up too much and that unless a warning was issued, inflation would return. As guardian of the integrity of the American dollar, he could not allow that to happen. So with great fanfare he increased the Federal Funds rate from 3 to 3¼ percent. Big deal, everybody thought. Well, everybody thought wrong. During the next twelve months, Greenspan raised rates six more times. This led to a near panic reaction in the world's financial markets, triggering a massive sell-off in bonds from New York to London to Frankfurt. The higher interest rates went, the more bond prices fell. It's no wonder, then, that by the end of 1994 Japanese investors were ready to start getting out. It's also no wonder that the Swiss and Germans who had suffered similar immense losses in their portfolios of American securities as a result of the depreciation of the dollar were starting to do the same thing. By 1995 foreigners had invested a total of well over a trillion dollars in American assets. And now some of them decided it was time to take their money and go home.

So at the beginning of February 1995—in a process triggered by the Mexican crisis and kept active by fears concerning Canada and Latin America—an unprecedented run on the U.S. dollar began. It sank like a rock against both the yen and the deutsche mark during the next 30 days. And the Great Dollar/Yen Crisis of 1995 was underway.

The question now was whether the central banks and treasuries of Japan, Germany, and especially the United States were willing, ready, and *able* to stop the run on the dollar before it undermined the entire global financial and trading system.

4

WHERE THE UNITED STATES WAS CONCERNED, it soon became clear that neither the U.S. Treasury nor the Federal Reserve was willing to step in to halt the fall in the dollar. The United States Treasury, acting through the Federal Reserve Bank of New York, could have intervened in the foreign exchange markets by buying in dollars for yen and marks and thus stabilizing the dollar's price. The Federal Reserve, acting on its own, could have raised short-term interest rates in the United States, thus increasing the attractiveness of dollar bank deposits or short-term U.S. government notes. But neither chose to act.

There are those who are of the opinion that the United States government did not act because it was *deliberately* seeking to devalue the dollar in order to make American goods more competitive in world markets. This, they claim, amounted to nothing less than a revival of the "beggar-my-neighbor" policies of the 1930s when, at the height of the Great Depression, nation after nation went the route of competitive devaluation with disastrous results for the world economy.

Some went even further. Japan's transportation minister, Shizuka Kamei, was quoted as suggesting that America favored a weak dollar in order to enslave the Japanese, who had to work twice as hard in order to keep export levels high. He compared this modern servitude to America's prior enslavement of Africans. There is probably some truth to these allegations, although hardly along the lines that Kamei suggested. At the very least the United States was guilty of the same "benign neglect" that it admitted to perpetrating from 1985 to 1988, when the dollar was allowed to depreciate by 35 percent. There was a great difference between the two, however. During the first half of the 1980s extremely high American interest rates had attracted money from all over the world, a process that pushed up the exchange value of the dollar. Even the value of the Yen fell from 180 to 260 to the dollar during this period. In terms of relative purchasing power the dollar had become greatly overvalued. So there was a strong case at that time for "benign neglect."

At the beginning of 1995 there was no such case. The dollar was now anything but overvalued. The Paris-based OECD (Organization for Economic Cooperation and Development), as neutral an observer as you could ask for, calculated that according to average purchasing power, at the end of 1994 the dollar was "worth" 181 yen, as compared to the market rate of around 100 to the dollar. As already mentioned, however, during the 1990s the current account deficits of the United States had been growing at an alarming rate, making such calculations of purchasing power parities irrelevant. Further devaluation of the dollar was one way to correct this. To be sure, historical evidence seemed to show that devaluations almost always had a very negative side effect, namely inflation. But many American experts in this area felt that this danger was not nearly as great as had been assumed. Harvard professor Martin Feldstein, who had been one of President Reagan's principle economic advisors during the last period of dollar devaluation, wrote the following:

> Even during the dollar's sharp 35% fall from 1985 to 1988, the rate of inflation was only 3.1%, actually less than it had been in the three prior years when the dollar rose by 23%.

He went on to say:

> The dollar's decline over the past decade has been a natural and inevitable response to the persistent U.S. trade deficits. Because a dollar decline does not induce an equally large offsetting rise in the prices of American tradable goods, a lower dollar makes American products more competitive in

world markets and thereby helps to shrink the U.S. trade deficit. In 1986 our current account deficit exceeded 3.5% of gross domestic product. The dollar's decline after 1985 cut that GDP share in half by 1990.[1]

It's a natural conclusion that policymakers in the 1995 White House and Treasury Department—despite the fact that they were Democrats while Feldstein is a Republican—accepted his thesis that the dollar's decline was "natural and inevitable" and that there was really nothing to fear where inflation was concerned.

If this reasoning is sound, then there was also no case to be made for the United States Treasury's intervention in foreign exchange markets in 1995—buying in dollars for yen or marks to boost the dollar's value. To be sure, it did make some efforts to placate the criticism coming out of Tokyo and Bonn, but the amounts involved in these token interventions never amounted to anything sizeable. This reticence no doubt also stemmed from a recognition that there was increasing evidence this type of intervention no longer worked. By 1995, the daily volume of foreign exchange transaction had reached $1 *trillion* dollars. What good could even *combined* central bank intervention do to turn the tide, asked the more cynical observers, since it never involved more than a couple billion dollars at a time? Besides, the more cynical observers might add, since the Treasury had already committed $20 billion of its Exchange Stabilization Fund to shore up the Mexican peso, it had only $16 billion left to support the dollar.

The other classical way to defend a currency under attack is for the central bank of the country under siege to raise short-term interest rates. In order to be effective, however, rates must be raised dramatically. Mexico provided an extreme example of this. After the bailout package was in place in early 1985, short-term interest rates in Mexico were pushed up to 60 percent per annum. Two months later, money started to flow back into Mexico.

Where the United States was concerned, such drastic measures were hardly called for. A one percent increase in short-term dollar interest rates in March 1995 would probably have sufficed to stop the plunge in the dollar. However, if the Federal Reserve had done this, it would have come under severe criticism from all quarters within the United States. This criticism would have been correctly placed since still higher interest rates could very well have dumped the American economy into a recession in the second half of 1995.

In 1995, the American economy found itself in a very delicate phase of the business cycle. It had been brought to this stage by monetary policy, under which the Federal Reserve adjusts the money supply and short-term interest rates with the dual aim of altering the pace of economic growth and curbing inflation. It raises interest rates when it is trying to slow an overheated economy in order to prevent a rise in the rate of inflation. It lowers interest rates when it feels that the economy is headed into a recession and requires the stimulus that lower rates will provide in the form of an incentive for people to borrow in order to buy houses or cars. As already mentioned, between February 1994 and February 1995, the Federal Reserve raised short-term interest rates *seven* times. The rate that the Federal Reserve manipulates is the Federal Funds rate at which banks borrow from each other on an overnight basis. It does so by intervening in the market for U.S. government securities. When it wants interest rates to go down, it buys securities, thus adding liquidity to the system. When it wants interest rates to go up, it sells.

In its meeting in March 1995, the Open Market Committee of the Federal Reserve, the body that makes these decisions, decided to neither buy nor sell—that enough was enough. It was now going to stand pat and hold the Federal Funds rate at 6 percent despite what was happening to the value of the dollar abroad. The Open Market Committee made this decision because by March 1995 the American economy was definitely beginning to slow down, having just finished a strong year. The overall economy had grown at the unexpectedly high rate of over 4 percent. The rate of inflation had fallen to 2.7 percent, the lowest rate in recent memory.

And unemployment had dropped to 5.4 percent, one of the lowest rates in decades.

Eventually, however, the much higher interest rates that the Fed had engineered started to take effect. As a result of much higher mortgage rates, home buyers were reluctant to buy houses, so both the sale of existing homes and the construction of new homes had fallen dramatically. Vehicle sales, which had been taking place at a record pace in 1994, now began to slow as well, the high cost of financing their purchase playing an important role. Retail sales were also beginning to slump, the fact that consumers had to pay 18 percent interest on their credit card balances certainly was partly to blame.

If, under these conditions, the Federal Reserve had continued to raise rates, there would have been serious concerns that recession would follow. To be sure, the primary task of the Federal Reserve is to preserve the integrity of the dollar—at least its *domestic* integrity—by holding down the rate of inflation. But the threat of an imminent return of inflation was simply not a serious one in 1995. It was not just that the wholesale and consumer price indices continued to show annual increases in the acceptable range of 3 percent. (Alan Greenspan correctly says that relying on such indices is like looking in a rear- view mirror.) What was equally important was what was happening to two key commodity prices—oil and gold—and what the trend was in wages relative to worker productivity.

The price of crude oil had stayed in the $20-per-barrel range, as compared to twice that much in the late 1970s, when oil prices triggered an upward spike in inflation that ultimately led to killer interest rates that dumped the United States into deep recession in the early 1980s. The same was true of gold prices, which remained stuck below $400 an ounce despite the dollar problem as compared to $800 an ounce back when inflation was on its way to double digits.

Wages, which represented 70 percent of total business costs in the United States, were also under control. Labor costs in 1994 had risen at the lowest annual rate in 30 years—only 2.4

percent. The low rise in labor costs occurred while American productivity continued to increase dramatically, meaning that Americans were actually producing many goods with less expense in 1995 than they had a year earlier. By March 1995, the outlook for inflation was even more favorable since overall economic growth was progressively slowing.

The objective of monetary policy at this point in time had then shifted from fighting inflation to making sure that growth continued to slow, but did not stop, or even worse, go into reverse. The only sound monetary policy was to leave interest rates alone. And that is precisely what the Fed did.

So if, from the American point of view, both intervention in the currency markets and higher interest rates were out of the question, what option remained? The only feasible option was a policy change that would not have any real effect in the short run but could have a fundamental effect on the dollar's international status in the long run. That was the fiscal policy of the United States. As early as 1987 a Japanese observer, J. Wakasugi, had summed up the importance of this:

> The fundamental causes of the dollar's depreciation are the U.S. budget deficit and an unfavorable balance of payments which shows no sign of improving. Only the U.S. itself can recover the dollar's status as an international key currency. Therefore, in the long run, decreasing the budget deficit and enhancing productivity are vital steps.[2]

An American observer, Professor Paul McCracken, a former member of the President's Council of Economic Advisors, came to the same conclusion in early 1995:

> Why would the currency of a country turning in this kind of a solid, orderly and essentially noninflationary economic expansion be getting such a vote of no confidence in the international financial community?

If we laid out the facts of the U.S. economy before a committee of experts, disguising the country's identity, the diagnosis and prescription would be quite predictable. They would probably conclude that the problem was the fiscal policies of the government. In 12 of the past 15 years, for example, the U.S. budget deficit has exceeded the European Union's target upper limit of 3% of gross domestic product. The ratio of the country's public debt to its GDP has doubled in the past 15 years and now exceeds 70%, well above the European Union's target upper limit of 60%. Moreover, the government's own long-range budget estimates (often optimistic) project a continued rise in this ratio for the rest of the decade.[3]

As Professor McCracken said, the outlook was that the United States would continue to run deficits indefinitely. The 1995 Clinton budget foresaw deficits of at least $200 billion a year for the next three years, after which they would again begin to climb rapidly.

But by March 1995, Clinton was no longer really in charge of the financial affairs of the United States. As a result of the Republican victory in the November 1994 elections, it was the Republicans, under the leadership of Newt Gingrich, the speaker of the House of Representatives, who were now setting the national agenda. And right on the top of that agenda was balancing the budget. Gingrich's program had been laid out in the so-called Contract with America, which listed ten pieces of legislation that he pledged to pass during the first 100 days of a Republican-controlled Congress. One of these was an amendment to the United States Constitution that would require that the national budget be balanced in the year 2002 and then stay balanced unless there was some unforeseen economic crisis. Amending the American Constitution is not easy. It requires that in both the lower house, the House of Representatives, and the upper house, the United States Senate, a proposed amendment be approved by two-thirds of its

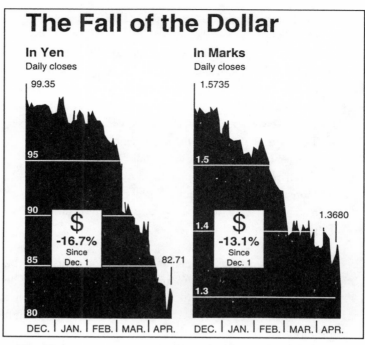

Figure 4.1

members. Then it is sent on to each of the 50 states for approval by their legislatures.

The amendment had easily passed in the House of Representatives. The big hurdle would now be the Senate. It was extremely close, but in a vote on March 3, 1995, the amendment failed to pass by two votes.

This was the third strike where the dollar was concerned. So the value of the dollar plunged down yet again. The climax was reached on April 19, 1995 when, for a very brief period, one dollar would get you only 79 Yen.

What one was now seeing in the foreign exchange markets came very close to panic selling of the dollar. And its coming immediately after the Senate's rejection of the balanced-budget amendment was considered by many observers to be hardly coincidental. Which brings us back to an earlier question. What was behind this currency crisis in 1995?

The Japanese answer was blunt. The fault clearly lay with America. The cure was equally clear: America must put its fiscal house in order.

5

MOST AMERICANS WOULD DISAGREE with the Japanese assessment of blame, saying that it was the rising yen, not the falling dollar, that was the problem. As the yen rose in value through the cross-exchange-rates mechanism (where yen and mark are traded directly with each other, and not through the dollar), it "pulled" the deutsche mark up with it. The deutsche mark, in turn, then pulled up its "satellite" currencies, such as the Dutch guilder and the Swiss franc. It was only against the yen and the deutsche mark that the dollar had fallen. When measured in global terms, the dollar had remained firm.

Some analysts would seek to bolster this global argument by using gold as a benchmark to assess what happened in the currency markets. Two Boston economists, Marc Miles and Richard Salsman, put it this way:

> The dollar hasn't fallen through the floor. Rather, the yen (and the German mark) have broken through the ceiling. How can you tell? In terms of an objective measure of purchasing power such as gold, the dollar has been quite stable over the past year and a half. The gold price solves the paradox of a "weak" dollar accompanying bullish U.S. stock and bond markets.
>
> Meanwhile, the yen price of gold has moved downward, falling precipitously. The yen is appreciating steadily against gold (the yen buys more gold). The dollar has not been falling over the past year—it is the yen that's been deflating.[1]

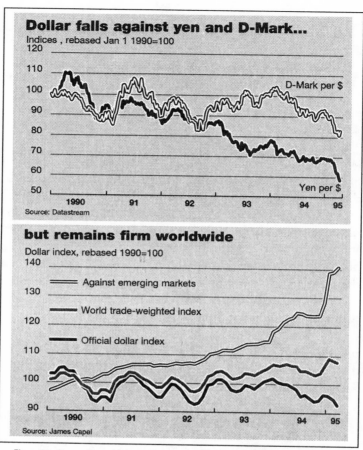

Dollar falls against yen and D-Mark...

Indices , rebased Jan 1 1990=100

D-Mark per $

Yen per $

Source: Datastream

but remains firm worldwide

Dollar index, rebased 1990=100

Against emerging markets

World trade-weighted index

Official dollar index

Source: James Capel

Figure 5.1 Source: Samuel Brittan, "Rival Yardsticks for the Dollar," *The Financial Times,* April 13, 1995, p. 20. Reprinted by permission of *The Financial Times.* © 1995. All Rights Reserved Worldwide.

In addition, the meteoric rise in the value of the yen during the first four months of 1995 was nothing new. It had been rising against the dollar—and all other currencies, for that matter—since the early 1970s, when the system of fixed exchange rates collapsed and was replaced by floating rates.

The cause for this rising yen was Japan's mercantilistic trading policies, under the aegis of MITI. These policies were the

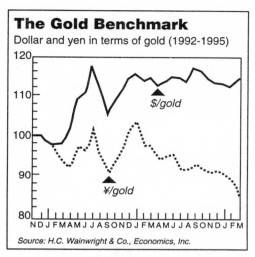

The Gold Benchmark

Dollar and yen in terms of gold (1992-1995)

$/gold

¥/gold

N D J F M A M J J A S O N D J F M A M J J A S O N D J F M

Source: H.C. Wainwright & Co., Economics, Inc.

Figure 5.2 Source: Marc A. Miles and Richard M. Salsman, "Why is the Dollar Falling? It Isn't," *The Wall Street Journal,* April 6, 1995, p. A16. Reprinted by permission of *The Wall Street Journal,* © 1995 Dow Jones & Company, Inc. All Rights Reserved Worldwide.

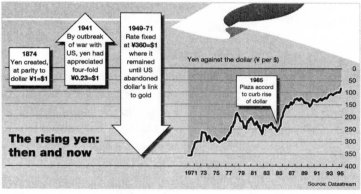

Figure 5.3 Source: William Dawkins, "History Reveals Wild Variation in Dollar/Yen Rate: Currency Reaches Dizzy New Heights," *The Financial Times,* April 20, 1995, p. 4. Reprinted by permission of *The Financial Times* © 1995. All Rights Reserved Worldwide.

force behind Japan's ever-larger trade surpluses, especially with the United States.

In particular, the United States had only a 2 percent share of the Japanese market for auto and auto parts whereas the

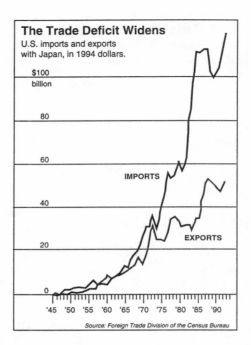

The Trade Deficit Widens
U.S. imports and exports
with Japan, in 1994 dollars.

IMPORTS

EXPORTS

$100 billion

80

60

40

20

0

'45 '50 '55 '60 '65 '70 '75 '80 '85 '90

Source: Foreign Trade Division of the Census Bureau

Figure 5.4

Japanese had a 24 percent share of the American market. The sale of cars and car parts accounted for nearly 60 percent of Japan's trade surplus with the United States. and almost one-quarter of America's entire worldwide deficit. Most Americans believe that unfair Japanese trade practices, epitomized by this gross imbalance in the vehicle trade, led to a shortage of yen in the world. This shortage inevitably led to a continuing rise in the price of the yen in terms of other currencies, especially against the dollar.

For the vast majority of the American public the cure for this problem was quite obvious: Reduce Japan's trade surplus (and thus America's trade deficit) by *forcing* Japan to buy more American-made cars and especially American-made car parts. This attitude was simplistic and, in the opinion of many, basically wrong. But it became the basis of U.S. government policy.

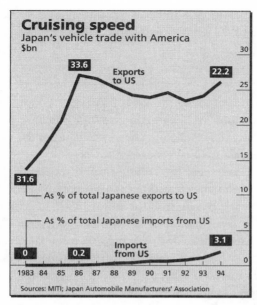

Figure 5.5 Source: *The Economist*, May 13, 1995. © 1995 The Economist Newspaper Group, Inc. Reprinted with permission. Further reproduction prohibited.

This policy of confrontation became concrete at 12:01 A.M., Saturday, May 20, 1995, when a prohibitive 100 percent import tariff was evoked (announced, though not yet imposed) on 13 models of luxury cars made in Japan. Two hundred thousand of these cars, valued at almost $6 billion, had been exported annually to the United States. These prohibitive tariffs would be rescinded only if Japan acceded to American demands that Japanese automobile companies use a much higher percentage of American-made parts in vehicles manufactured in Japan. Japan, of course, rejected these demands, claiming that they violated the basic principles agreed to by both countries under the General Agreement on Tariffs and Trade (GATT). Both appealed to GATT's successor, the new World Trade Organization (WTO).

At the last minute, an agreement was reached in Geneva between the two chief negotiators, Japan's Ryutaro Hashimoto, and America's Mickey Kantor. It had three basic elements: (1) deregulation of the replacement parts market in Japan, allowing for higher sales in Japan of parts made in the United States; (2) improved access of America manufacturers to Japanese dealerships; and (3) plans by the five largest Japanese car producers to increase their purchases of North American parts, expand vehicle production in North America and purchase American parts for production in Japan. The key element of the three was the last: Japanese car makers agreed to increase their purchases of American parts by $9 billion over three years. But the Japanese government stressed that this was purely a voluntary agreement, made by the private sector, with no government guarantees of performance. This led many American observers to strongly criticize the "deal," saying that it fell far short of the expectations raised by the Clinton administration. That prompted London's *Financial Times* to suggest that "further conflicts appear ineluctable."

This episode raised extremely difficult questions about the entire American-Japanese relationship, which had now become more fragile than at any time in postwar history. At stake, ultimately, was an alliance that had been at the core of a "Pax Pacifica," whereby a fire wall would be maintained by the United States between money matters and other elements of the alliance. The *New York Times* has described this fire wall as:

> the assurance that trade issues will never get mixed up with the rest of the relationship, particularly America's huge and lopsided security guarantees for Japan. Those accords— from the nuclear umbrella to the 35-year-old Mutual Security Treaty—have been the linchpin of the Pacific in modern times, assuring America a role as the power-balancer in Asia, and at once making the world free for Japanese trade. . . .[2]

But how much longer could this fire wall remain intact? In answering that question the *Times* cited Jeffrey Garten, the under secretary of commerce for trade, who said, "Over a long period of time, absent an identifiable enemy, there is no precedent in history for strong security ties in the face of a highly unbalanced economic and commercial relationship."

Despite these ominous rumblings, Japan is not about to be convinced. In recent polls only 12 percent of Japanese were willing to concede that their trade policies might be unfair. Eighty-five percent believe that America unfairly blames Japan for its trade deficits. So if these positions remain irreconcilable, what path will the future take?

- Will the value of the yen once again increase as the value of the dollar sinks lower?
- If the above comes to pass, what would that mean for the dollar as a reserve currency?
- What would a still higher yen and a still lower dollar mean for the financial markets in New York and Tokyo?
- What would be the impact on the Japanese and American economies?
- Could all this lead to a global financial and economic crisis?

Let's seek the answers to these questions within the framework of a "worst case scenario."

Part II

6

PESSIMISTS SAY that even if Japan partially caves in to Americans' demands and pledges to increase its imports of American-made car parts by $9 billion over three years, the effect on the American trade deficit will be negligible. The overall annual current account deficit (defined as the sum of trade in goods and services, investment income, and government grants), for example, which totalled $152 billion in both 1994 and 1995, would be reduced by a mere 6 percent. This would hardly result in any dramatic turnaround in the fortunes of either the dollar or the yen. In fact, one of America's leading experts on matters of international trade, William Cline, an economist with the Institute for International Economics, predicts that the American deficit will not remain at $152 billion but will balloon to $200 billion and remain there for several years. His research findings indicate that the dollar's decline in 1995 was the result of the trade deficit rather than merely a whim of the financial markets. Implicit in all this is that a renewed fall in the exchange value of the dollar is inevitable. Cline concludes that the United States is travelling down a dangerous path that could lead to economic downfall. Another highly respected American economist, C. Fred Bergsten, holds the same opinion. "When you let your trade deficit go up like this," he wrote in the *Wall Street Journal,* "you're really setting your economy up for a collapse. We know from history that we cannot sustain a huge trade deficit."[1] Bergsten cites Mexico as the most recent example of what inevitably happens to nations who allow their trade deficits to get out of control.

Doesn't such a statement, though, ignore the possible impact on that trade deficit of a dramatic change in American fiscal policy? Although the Republicans in Congress and President Clinton failed to reach an agreement in 1996 on a long-term budget plan, each side committed to achieving a balanced budget by the year 2002. They continue to disagree about the extent to which growth in entitlements spending will be cut back, and the nature and size of future tax cuts. But even these differences are not great. The odds are very high that eventually a long-term budget plan will be put in place. Will this not result in a dramatic reduction in our trade deficit?

No, say some experts. They explain that even now, when the United States is finally embarking upon a course that will lead to a balanced budget by the year 2002, the initial effect on the dollar could very well turn out to be exactly the opposite of what is expected. Before things get better, they tell us, it is highly likely that the dollar will once again start to go down. The yen, which in 1996 retraced some of its earlier rise from 79 to the dollar, temporarily settling in the range of 105-110 to the dollar, would once again start to move up.

One of these experts is Harvard professor Martin Feldstein, who writes:

> As Congress begins in earnest to tackle the tough but vital task of reducing the budget deficit, there are widespread but false assertions that a lower U.S. budget deficit would raise the dollar's value relative to other currencies. The finance ministers of Germany, France and Japan, as well as the head of the International Monetary Fund, have all urged the U.S. to cut the budget deficit in order to reverse the dollar's recent decline. It's very puzzling that some of the same officials who a decade ago urged the U.S. to cut its budget deficit in order to *reduce* the value of the dollar are now urging us to cut our deficit in order to *raise* the dollar's value. . . .
>
> In fact, however, both our own past experience and basic economic analysis imply the opposite: The likely response to deficit reduction would actually be to *accelerate the dollar's decline.*

The reasoning is this:

> Some of those who assert that a lower budget deficit would
> raise the dollar argue along the following lines: (A) The large
> trade deficit is causing the dollar to decline. (B) The trade
> deficit is equal to the difference between national investment
> and national saving. (C) Reducing the budget deficit would
> raise national saving. (D) The higher level of saving would
> reduce the trade deficit. (E) Since the large trade deficit is
> causing the dollar to decline, the lower trade deficit brought
> about by the higher level of saving would cause the value of
> the dollar to rise. The logical error in this argument comes in
> going from (D) to (E). While an increase in demand for U.S.
> products that follows lower trade barriers abroad or higher
> trade barriers in the U.S. would raise the value of the dollar,
> the decline of the trade deficit that results from a higher level
> of saving *occurs only because it lowers the value of the dollar.*[2]

Another highly respected American authority, Stanford professor
Paul Krugman, comes to the same conclusion in his book,
Currencies and Crises:

> It is highly likely that when fiscal policy finally is fixed,
> further real depreciation by the United States and further
> real appreciation by the surplus countries will be required.
> It would therefore be a mistake if exchange rates were to be
> fixed at current levels, on the basis of a misguided belief that
> fiscal policy somehow fixes trade imbalances without real
> exchange rate changes.[3]

Krugman expanded on this in a recent article in the *Financial
Times.* He begins by pointing out that it is almost universally
accepted by finance ministers, central bankers, and the markets
that the key to strengthening the dollar is to increase the U.S.
savings rate. This, orthodoxy contends, could be best accom-
plished by eliminating the budget deficit. He suggests that in

economics, as in life, a little knowledge can be a dangerous thing. We are dealing here, he claims, with "the doctrine of immaculate transfer," a phrase coined by another economist, John Williamson.

> It is a fact of accounting that the surplus or deficit on any nation's balance of payments on current account is precisely equal to the difference between national savings and national investment. It is therefore reasonable to expect an increase in savings to be reflected in a reduced trade deficit. It is also true that foreign exchange markets often—though not always—react to good news about the trade balance by bidding up a currency.
>
> So the story seems clear: a higher savings rate will mean a better US trade balance, which in turn means a stronger dollar. What could possibly be wrong with this analysis?
>
> The problem becomes apparent if one asks *how* a higher savings rate translates into a smaller trade deficit. It is not enough to insist that the accounting ensures that it must. A consumer deciding between a Ford and a Honda cares nothing about the US's national income accounts. How does a lower US budget deficit persuade Americans to buy fewer foreign goods and foreigners to buy more US products?

Obviously it does not. Then what *does* induce people to switch to U.S. goods? The answer is that higher savings will normally reduce the trade deficit only because they result in a *weaker* dollar.

> The chain of events would look something like this: a fall in the budget deficit reduces demand in the US economy; to avoid a recession, the Federal Reserve lowers interest rates; as a result, the dollar falls: this lower dollar makes US goods cheaper compared with foreign substitutes, causing the necessary switch in expenditure.

Krugman claims that such a sequence demonstrates how naive it is to think that government financial balance changes will also change physical trade flows "without working through a mechanism such as the exchange rate."

This belief in "immaculate transfer" is mistaken, he argues, and it confuses "the accounting principle which says that the current account balance equals the savings-investment balance with the process that enforces that constraint on decision-makers."[4]

Krugman contends that it is hard to argue with the view that countries should rely on changing currency values rather than deflation and inflation to achieve the real exchange rate changes that are needed to correct external imbalances. He cites Nobel laureate Milton Friedman, who made the analogy with changing to daylight savings time: Just as it is easier for people to set their clocks back an hour than to change their schedules, it is easier to change one price—the exchange rate—than to change the prices of all individual products. So, these experts conclude, despite the United States imposing trade sanctions on Japan, and despite (or, rather, because of) the fact that the United States is finally moving in the right direction where fiscal policy is concerned, a further depreciation of the dollar seems inevitable.

There are observers who look at the same problem from the yen side and come to an equally pessimistic conclusion. George Magnus, the chief economist of the British merchant banking firm S. G. Warburg, has claimed that the Japanese have become trapped in a vicious cycle of deflation that dates back to 1990 when the Bank of Japan attacked inflated asset values. According to another economist, Carl Weinberg, chief economist at the New York–based High Frequency Economics, the Bank of Japan did such a good job of bursting the "bubble economy" that it accidentally also destroyed the entire collateral base for bank lending.

This continuing unwillingness of Japanese banks to lend puts more pressure on Japanese companies and institutions to bring | 5 1 money into Japan in order to shore up their own damaged balance sheets, according to a third economist, Ravi Bulchandani of Morgan Stanley. As a result, these companies sell overseas assets (such as in the case of Matsushita's sale of MCA) and repatriate the funds, creating an even greater demand for yen that makes the currency appreciate still faster. Just as the threat of future inflation can weaken a currency's value, so the anticipation of further deflation can strengthen a currency. (In this context, it is interesting to note that in its most recent forecasts, the Paris-based OECD sees Japanese prices declining further throughout all of 1996 and well into 1997.)

So we have heard several voices all saying the same thing: Despite the historic agreement to balance the U.S. budget by the year 2002, and despite the dollar's partial recovery from under 80 to well over 100 yen to the dollar, the dollar will fall—and the yen will rise—again. If they are right, where could the dollar/yen exchange rate end up before this process ends? Most academics are extremely reluctant to even hazard a guess. But in the financial community there is an unofficial consensus that it would be in the range of 90 to 95 yen to the dollar.

7

THIS BRINGS US TO THE POSSIBLE THIRD STAGE in this currency saga. The first was the trigger—the Mexican peso crisis. The second was the run on the dollar, led by the world's speculators. The third could be what we will term "the portfolio crisis." A "portfolio crisis" would arise if enough of the institutions that own dollar-denominated assets believe the pessimistic view of the future of the dollar and try to sell their dollar assets before it happens.

This raises the question of how much is in "safe" hands. On the surface it appears that a large proportion is in very "responsible" hands, namely those people who run the world's central banks. In recent years, they have been accumulating dollars at a very rapid rate as they bought them in order to prevent their currencies from rising even further than they already have. It is estimated that total foreign exchange reserves of the world's central banks now total $1.3 trillion. Most of these dollars (nearly $900 billion) are then invested in U.S. government bonds and notes.

The fact that this central bank buying accelerated tremendously as a result of the currency crisis is one reason for the sharp rise in U.S. bond prices during 1995. Since this bond rally pulled up stock prices, as bond rallies almost always do, this phenomenon also goes far in explaining why the Dow Jones Industrial Average (DJIA) rose 34 percent in 1995, one of its best years ever. It could also suggest, however, that what happened in 1995 as a result of the dollar/yen currency crisis was the creation of a bubble in the U.S. securities market.

The vulnerability of this American bubble was indicated by the only big interruption in the great bull market of 1995. In the middle of May, the DJIA dropped over 2 percent in one day,

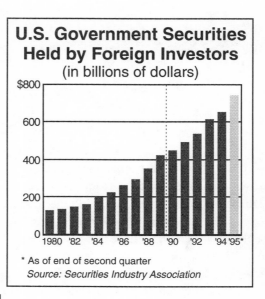

**U.S. Government Securities
Held by Foreign Investors**
(in billions of dollars)

* As of end of second quarter
Source: Securities Industry Association

Figure 7.1

the result of rumors that the Bank of England was starting to unload part of its portfolio of U.S. government bonds. These rumors proved false. But the point was made.

The problem, however, does not lie with the Bank of England or the Bank of Japan. The potential problem lies with the central banks of the developing countries, especially the newly rich Asian countries such as Taiwan and Singapore. Six of the world's ten biggest holders of foreign exchange reserves are now emerging countries, five of which are in Asia. Together they control over half of the world's total reserves.

How truly safe are these reserves? Not very, some currency traders say, claiming that it was precisely dollar selling and yen buying by some of some central banks that contributed to the panic in April 1995, which drove the yen/dollar exchange rate to 79.

There is, though, a more general issue at stake, namely the role of the dollar as a reserve currency and the international

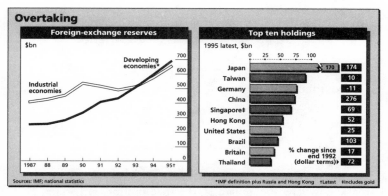

Figure 7.2 Source: *The Economist*, November 18, 1995. © 1995 The Economist Newspaper Group, Inc. Reprinted with permission. Further reproduction prohibited.

responsibilities of those who are supposed to be the guardians of the integrity of that currency. Professor Paul Krugman in his book, *Currencies and Crises,* summed up the role of a reserve currency by assigning it six functions (see table 7.1). He explains them as follows:

> The dollar is used as a medium of exchange in private transactions, or "vehicle," and is also bought and sold by central banks, thus making it an "intervention" currency. Trade contracts are sometimes denominated in dollars, making it an "invoice" currency, and the par values for exchange rates are sometimes stated in terms of the dollar, which makes it serve as a "peg." Finally, private agents hold liquid dollar-denominated assets—the "banking" role— and central banks hold the dollar as a reserve.

Krugman adds this qualification, however: "central banks of small countries may behave more like private agents than like Group of Ten monetary authorities."[1] This is an important distinction, and we shall return to it later. First, however, let's focus on the key functions of the dollar as a reserve currency, starting with its role as a "vehicle."

TABLE 7.1

Roles of an International Currency

	PRIVATE	OFFICIAL
Medium of exchange	Vehicle	Intervention
Unit of account	Invoice	Peg
Store of value	Banking	Reserve

The dollar's special role as a vehicle is in the interbank market, where the dollar is *the* medium of exchange. As J. Kubarych has pointed out, virtually all interbank transactions involve a purchase or sale of dollars for a foreign currency. This is true even if a bank's aim is to buy German marks for pounds sterling. Because the dollar is the main currency in international trade and investment, the dollar market for each of the world's currencies is much more active than between any pair of foreign currencies. By going through the dollar, large amounts can be traded more easily.

The dollar also plays a key role as an international unit of account. Often in international trade sellers prefer to invoice in the currency of the larger country. So the dollar, as the currency of the United States, the world's largest economy, is used disproportionately for invoicing in export transactions to the United States. For example, most of Japanese or Canadian exports to the United States are invoiced in U.S. dollars. In addition, raw material trade—such as trade in oil—is also invoiced in dollars, even though that trade might not involve the United States, since it is easier for exporters of such primary products to have all contracts throughout the world written in the same currency.

Charles Kindelberger has used the analogy between money and language to explain the international role of the dollar as a unit of account. If I want to communicate with someone of a different nationality, one or both of us must learn a second language. If you were from a small country like

Luxembourg, and I was from a large one like Germany, you would probably have to learn German. It would follow that if we made a business deal with each other, it would probably be in marks. But if we were both from a small country, or one with an "obscure" language, we would both use an international language. This explains why, when a businessman from Holland deals with a Brazilian, or a Japanese with a Russian, they probably talk in English and negotiate in dollars. This also applies to a certain degree to capital markets. Adjustable rate mortgages in California are tied to the London Interbank Lending Rate (LIBOR); both appear in dollars. Commodity futures traded on the Chicago Board of Trade, financial futures traded on the London International Financial Futures Exchange (LIFFE) in London, gold traded in Zurich—all are quoted in the common language of the dollar.

Where these functions are concerned, therefore, there are obviously good reasons for having one reserve currency and that—given the United States' dominant position in the world— that reserve currency be the dollar. But the case for the dollar as *the* reserve currency, as an international store of value, is increasingly less compelling. Because, as so many have found out, holding dollars these days is a very risky business.

Holding dollars would have involved no foreign exchange risk prior to 1971, when the dollar was pegged to gold and the yen, mark and franc were pegged to the dollar. But at the beginning of the 1970s, the United States had no choice but to no longer allow the central banks of the world to cash in their rising hoard of American dollars for their share of America's gold. Otherwise Fort Knox would have been emptied out. This decision to "close the gold window" meant that the world was now moving into uncharted waters: The era of floating exchange rates had begun, and the "good old days," when the businessmen of the world could wake up each morning confident that one dollar was worth 360 yen, 4 marks, and 4.3 Swiss francs, were over. And it only got worse. In 1995, Japanese businessmen woke up to find that the dollar they had received yesterday that was

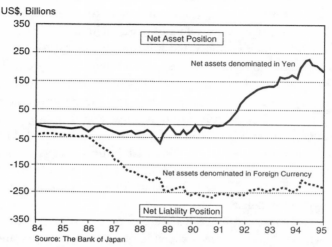

JAPAN SHIFTS DOLLAR RISK TO FOREIGNERS
Japanese Short-Term External Net Assets (Liabilities)
Held by Japanese Authorized Foreign Exchange Banks

US$, Billions

Net Asset Position

Net assets denominated in Yen

Net assets denominated in Foreign Currency

Net Liability Position

Source: The Bank of Japan

Figure 7.3 Source: Merrill Lynch Global Economics and Currencies, February 8, 1995. Reprinted by permission. Copyright © 1995 Merrill Lynch, Pierce, Fenner & Smith Incorporated.

worth 100 yen would now fetch only 97 yen. The morning after that it was down to 95.

So in recent years the dollar has proven to be anything but a store of value, and it is the Japanese who have suffered most. Although the Germans, Swiss, and Dutch have all had big losses, the Japanese have since 1980 suffered a foreign exchange loss of 600 billion dollars on their holdings of U.S. dollars. In the face of this, there can be no doubt that heavy damage has been inflicted on the dollar's reserve currency status.

Belgian economist Robert Triffin predicted this trend years ago.[2] He said that it is the fate of a reserve currency to grow weak with time. As its stock piles up around the world, diversification into other currencies or gold is bound to happen. And so it has with the dollar. The share of dollars in total world foreign exchange reserves has gradually sunk from 73 percent at the beginning of the 1980s to 62 percent today. Is the time near at hand when this slow move toward diversification may accelerate? Perhaps. And as the central banks of the world diversify their portfolios, they will purchase principally marks and yen, which will push up the price of the yen and the mark and push the exchange value of the dollar down, which is hardly what the world needs at the moment. Because of the dangers inherent in any flight from the dollar, the central banks of the most powerful countries of the world—those in the Group of Ten—will move very carefully where diversification is concerned. But it is the central banks of other countries—many of them small countries in the developing world—that now own the majority of the world's reserves. Now Krugman's comment—"central banks of small countries may behave more like private agents than like Group of Ten monetary authorities"—becomes relevant.

Some conclude that, if push comes to shove, these smaller countries will get out of the dollar and not worry about the consequences. If this precipitated a crisis in the "system," it would be up to the "monetary authorities" of the Group of Ten to take care of it. The Asian countries would do this because of a dramatic shift in the nature of international bank lending in Asia. The big lenders are, of course, Japanese banks. The big borrowers are businesses in Indonesia, Korea, Malaysia, the Philippines, and Thailand. In the past, as often as not, these loans were denominated in dollars. But during the past four years, new loans have been made in yen. Within a very short time, the net assets of Japanese Authorized Foreign Exchange Banks exploded from zero in 1991 to the yen equivalent of $250 billion in 1995. As a result, the share of the yen in the long-term debt of countries such as Indonesia, Malaysia, and the Philippines has risen to near 40 percent—in the case of Thailand, to over 50 percent. For all these countries, their foreign exchange reserves are in dollars, while their debt is in yen. When the dollar collapsed and the yen soared in value in 1995, it created enormous problems for these countries. This is why in March and April 1995, as the cost of the yen they would need to repay these debts was rising almost every

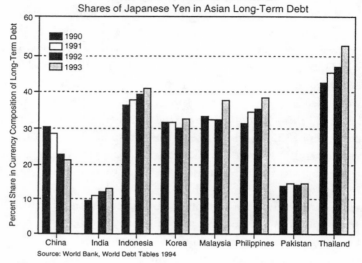

The Yen Rises in the East

Shares of Japanese Yen in Asian Long-Term Debt

Percent Share in Currency Composition of Long-Term Debt

- ■ 1990
- □ 1991
- ■ 1992
- ▨ 1993

China India Indonesia Korea Malaysia Philippines Pakistan Thailand

Source: World Bank, World Debt Tables 1994

Figure 7.4 Source: Merrill Lynch Global Economics and Currencies, February 8, 1995. Reprinted by permission. Copyright © 1995 Merrill Lynch, Pierce, Fenner & Smith Incorporated

day, they were frantically dumping dollars for yen, in essence, "covering" their short positions. The problem is that since their export income is still in dollars, while their mounting long-term debts are now denominated in yen, those short positions are increasing every month. If the dollar headed for another dive in the future, they could hardly be blamed for breaking ranks with the "monetary authorities" and dumping their dollars by the billions, or even tens of billions. This mass dumping of dollars could be the beginning of an unanticipated unravelling of the dollar's role as the reserve currency. After all, it was assumed that small countries would have small reserves. In the early 1970s, when the world entered the era of floating exchange rates, who would have guessed that in 1995 *Taiwan* would have foreign exchange reserves of almost $100 billion? Or that tiny Singapore would have almost $60 billion?

In addition to the situation in Asia, there is another new major force at work in the world of international finance, namely that of private currency speculators. To be sure, such speculators have always been around, but until 1973, the pickings were generally poor. As long as the world was on the dollar exchange standard, with fixed rates, very few opportunities came along where a private speculator could bet on or against a currency in the forward markets and make really big money. There were, of course, exceptions. In the late summer of 1967 rumor began to fly that the United Kingdom was experiencing enormous balance of payments difficulties. The Swiss banks decided to do something about it by amassing huge short positions in sterling in the interbank market. When word of this got around, there was a run on sterling that left the British authorities no choice but to devalue the pound, lowering the fixed rate of exchange from $2.80 to $2.40. The Swiss banks made out like bandits and were known thereafter in the City of London as "the gnomes of Zurich."

Now that rates are floating, and especially now that the volatility in foreign exchange markets seems to be ever increasing, the opportunities to make a killing in foreign exchange are no longer a once-in-a-decade affair. Currency speculation has become the big game in town. The best example of the role now played by big-time speculators was provided by the Hungarian-American George Soros. In September 1992, Soros, operating through the hedge fund he controlled, built up a huge short position in the pound sterling. He calculated that Great Britain had put the pound into the European currency grid at an unrealistically high level—a level that would prove unsustainable. He was right. When the rest of the world caught up with him, a flight from sterling ensued, one that drove the pound down from $2.00 to $1.50 within a very short time. When Soros covered his short positions he was rumored to have made $1 billion. This, of course, attracted the attention of hedge fund managers from all over the world. Here was a market that offered both high volatility and enormous leverage. According to Barton Biggs of the investment bank Morgan Stanley, this attracted a whole new group of hedge fund managers. "Today, there are probably 50 or 60 or even 100 new guys thrashing around," he noted, "following the smart guys, . . . and churning up the fairways."[3] Hundreds more have done the same since.

What makes gambling in foreign exchange more attractive than gambling in, say, cocoa or pork bellies, is the fact that there is always a major player in the game who is interested in maintaining the status quo—the central bank of the country whose currency has been "put in play." Thus, in the case of Soros, the more he went short, the bigger the position the Bank of England took on the other side. In the end, this became a zero-sum game: When the Bank of England lost, the windfall gain to Soros came essentially from the public coffers. When one can tap the public coffers, one has deep pockets—the deepest pockets of all. This, in times past, gave the central banks of the world the upper hand. But today, when a Bankers Trust, a Union Bank of Switzerland, a Barings Brothers, and a Deutsche Bank join forces with hundreds of hedge funds—all operating independently but with the same objective—their combined power can overwhelm any central bank in the world.

Let's look closer at hedge funds and the role of financial derivatives in currency markets. Hedge funds have been around a long time. Originally they were small stock funds with a stated investment policy that allowed them to go both long (when they expected stock prices to go up), and short (when they thought they were about to go down), in contrast to most mutual funds, which stay exclusively long in stocks. This, theoretically, provided the flexibility necessary to take advantage of both bull and bear markets. Hedge funds flowered in the late 1960s when investors became skeptical about the overheated stock market that had developed then, but most folded in the bear market of 1973-74, when the track records of most of them reflected more volatility than profitability.

But in recent times a new breed of hedge funds has come along. They are almost always organized in the form of limited partnerships, they operate worldwide, and they invest in anything that promises to make a quick buck. More often than not they are restricted to just 99 "sophisticated" investors with an extremely high net worth. Some, like George Soros's Quantum fund, are open only to non-American investors to avoid having to register with the American Securities and Exchange Commission. Despite the sudden recent growth in the number of hedge funds, there are, according to Barton Biggs, probably only a dozen or so players "who truly know what they are doing," among these Soros, Michael Steinhardt, Julian Robertson, Paul Tudor Jones, and John Henry. In 1992, those who invested money with these men made out like bandits. For example, that year Soros's fund was up 67.5 percent, Steinhardt's 50 percent, Robertson's 27.2 percent. Much of this was made by betting on the devaluation of the pound sterling in 1992.

These men all returned to the scene in 1995. Many American observers have scoffed at the notion that they played an important role in pounding down the dollar and pushing up the yen and mark. But the facts speak otherwise. In the first ten days of March, according to the *Wall Street Journal,* Henry's $1.3 billion fund made profits of $130 million from currency speculation; Jones's fund raked in $50 million; and Robertson was up $150 million. Such profits in such a short time could have resulted only by maximizing leverage. This means that in 1995, with around $10 billion under management, Soros was able to amass a total firepower of $100 to $150 billion—more than the entire dollar reserves of the Bank of Japan at that time. If you then take the firepower of the other hedge fund managers who "truly know what they are doing" plus that of those who don't, it adds up to a considerable amount. Today there are 800 to 900 hedge funds operating worldwide. According to the International Monetary Fund, total hedge fund capital today is around $100 billion. Apply a conservative 10 to 1 leverage factor, and these funds can control $1 trillion. To be sure, hedge funds are probably the highest risk game human beings have yet invented. But in March and April 1995, it didn't matter if you knew what you were doing or not. You simply had to go short the dollar and long the yen and you earned the reputation of a genius.

But where do the hedge fund managers get this leverage? In the currency market in 1995, it was the banks that supplied most of the leverage, since the only market that has the liquidity able to support this level of gambling in currencies is the interbank forward market. As the director of foreign exchange trading at the Swiss Bank Corporation in New York put it, "If you are a real player, you have to deal in the interbank market," where trade goes on 24 hours a day, in bulk, and very, very quickly without distorting prices. It is, after all, a market with a turnover of *a trillion dollars a day.*

Hedge funds that use that interbank market get most of their money through borrowing from commercial banks. And often, the leverage they end up with is astronomical. If a hedge fund gets a line at bank A and then leverages 10 times, bank A will probably not know that it is also going to bank B, borrowing the same amount of money, and leveraging 20 times.

Derivatives also played a role, at times a major one, in the currency crisis of 1995. In fact, it was, of all people, George Soros who claimed that one type of financial derivative, the so-called "knockout option," was largely responsible for the dollar's steep fall against the yen and the mark in 1995. Knockout options, like any options, give the holder the right to trade an amount of currency at a set price for a specified period of time, but they are rendered worthless, or "knocked out," if the market hits an agreed-upon price barrier. They are attractive because the risk of being knocked out makes them cheaper than conventional options. Thus, for instance, you can buy an ordinary six-month "call" to buy yen at 90 to the dollar for about 3.34 percent, or $3.34 million, for every $100 million bet. A call option that knocks out if the yen goes to 96 costs only 1.34 percent, or half the cost of the straight call.

How did such special options affect what happened in 1995? David Hale, chief economist at Kemper Financial in Chicago, claims they played a big role. He says that many Japanese exporters and Japanese banks moved to hedge against the falling dollar with such knockout options because they were confident at the time that the dollar would fall no further than 95 yen. Once the dollar plunged through 95, they lost everything. Having lost their hedges, they then scrambled to cover their exposure by dumping dollars in the spot (cash) market, driving the yen up even further. Who sold them the options? The hedge funds.

But before we blame everything on the hedge funds, let's go back to the banks. Their role in all this was by no means restricted to their providing leverage to hedge funds. In fact, banks themselves were the biggest players in currency markets in 1995, just as they have always been. In the past, any banker who deserved his pinstriped suit would vehemently deny that his bank *ever* speculated for its own account in the foreign exchange markets. They always squared their positions each and every evening before closing for the day. That pretense has now been abandoned. Some of the biggest commercial banks in the world—and some of the best too—fully admit to occasionally making the *majority of their profits* from proprietary speculation. To be sure, we are not talking just about foreign exchange; bonds also play a major role here. But just like the gnomes of Zurich in 1967, it was the gnomes of New York, London, *and* Zurich who played the dominant role in the currency crisis of 1995. In 1967 it was the pound sterling that was taken to the cleaners; in 1995, it was the dollar. In 1967 it was the Union Bank of Switzerland, the Credit Suisse, and the Swiss Bank Corporation who were the big players. In 1995 these three were joined by Bankers Trust, Deutsche Bank, Chase Manhattan, Chemical, and dozens of other commercial banks.

Investment banks also joined this group. We now know that Baring Brothers had a penchant for taking big risks in futures markets, especially those involving Japan and the yen. Nicholas Leeson, a young 28-year-old trader in Baring's Singapore office, took speculative positions in the tens of billions of dollars in Tokyo and eventually lost $1.5 billion, wiping out the capital of Barings and forcing it into bankruptcy. The pain in the City of London was all the greater because Barings was the banker of the Queen and had, in fact, been serving British monarchs for well over two centuries. When all this began to trickle out, Leeson fled Singapore and headed for London, but was dumb enough to book his flight through Frankfurt, where he was promptly arrested. Eventually, he was extradited back to Singapore and given a six-and-a-half-year sentence for falsifying documents related to his "unauthorized" trading activities. At year's end, a local brewery issued a special lager with Leeson's name, his picture, and "$1.5 billion" on the label, which enjoyed brisk sales among the traders in Singapore's financial district celebrating both the New Year and the fact that they weren't also in jail. Many knew that but for the grace of God, they might have suffered the same fate.

Such "unauthorized" trading scandals crop up time and time again, usually under very murky circumstances. Invariably the management of the financial institution involved blames it all on "rogue" traders. Outside observers contribute the rise of such rogue traders in recent times to a system that pays traders low salaries but rewards their successes with bonuses that often run into seven digits. The reward for failure, by contrast, is a pink slip at the end of the year. So there is an ever-present incentive for traders to hide failures and exaggerate successes.

But everyone knows that it is not nearly as clear cut as all that. Traders cannot make huge profits without having huge funds at their disposal, which they then use to finance high-risk speculations. Quite often they use highly complex computerized trading programs, based on mathematical models that would have warmed the heart of Einstein. Needless to say, this stuff is way above the heads of most top managers of these institutions—a large percentage of whom do not even know how to run a simple PC. But these managers do know how to use their pencils to calculate return on capital, and they are fully cognizant of the fact that extraordinary returns on capital almost by definition involve extraordinary risks. When these "accidents" occur, the question is invariably asked: Who at the top knew what, and when? Almost as invariably, that question is never answered. The trader is hung out to dry, and everyone at the top stonewalls until the problem goes away. In the case of Barings, it was the trader who hung the bank out to dry.

But it is not just London banks that are involved in such high risk/high reward activities. One of the directors of Salomon Brothers in New York likened his investment bank to a "gambling casino with a restaurant out front. The casino"—the group doing proprietary trading—"is the thing we really want," he said, "because it makes a lot of money. And we are happy to have the restaurant"—consumer business such as stock and bond trading and investment banking—"as long as it doesn't cost too much." So it was all of these—hedge funds, commercial banks, and investment banks—that were, along with the "small country" central banks in Asia, the prime forces moving the foreign exchange markets in 1995. And all of them acted selfishly. The small countries in Asia were trying to hedge against the foreign exchange risk inherent in their earning dollars while owing yen. The hedge funds, the commercial banks, and the investment banks, by contrast, were out to make a very big buck in a very short time at somebody else's expense. They saw themselves as simply agents of inevitable free market forces.

If future circumstances put these "market forces" back in play, what kind of havoc could these "agents" wreak next time? Paul Krugman, in *Currencies and Crises*, describes what could happen this way:

> Suppose that international investors were suddenly to lose confidence in the United States. What it means to "lose confidence" is a slightly problematic issue; perhaps investors start to demand a risk premium on U.S. assets, perhaps they revise downward their views about the long-run equilibrium real exchange rate, or perhaps they start to have a "peso problem," viewing a catastrophic fall in the dollar as a possibility though not a probability. Whatever the precise nature of the loss of confidence, the important point is that

we suppose that investors become unwilling to hold claims on the United States at their current rates of return.

. . . Investors cannot simply pull their money out of the United States, since there would be nobody on the other side of the transaction. When everybody wants to sell, the result is not a lot of sales, but a fall in the price. *The immediate result of a loss of confidence in the United States then is not a sudden flight of capital but a sudden fall in the dollar.*[4]

What could cause investors to once again lose confidence in the dollar? Historically, the loss of investor confidence in a nation and its currency has had diverse origins. When this happened in Mexico recently, at least partial blame rested on the assassination of the man who was expected to be the nation's next president. In Europe, in countries like Italy, and in Latin America, this likewise occurs for internal political reasons.

External shocks can also be a cause. Most people forget what happened to the dollar as a result of the 1973 oil embargo, when the price of oil quadrupled overnight. It appeared to the world that this would usher in a major economic crisis in the United States, so many investors got out of the dollar and into other currencies. Within an extremely short time, the dollar fell from 3.25 Swiss francs to just 1.80, from 3 deutsche marks to 1.75, and from 350 yen to 250, sometimes changing more in two hours than they had in the previous two decades. At the bottom of the market in 1973, the rates at which you could buy dollars—at least where the European currencies were concerned—were, at least temporarily, not that different from the exchange rates that prevailed two decades later. In 1994, most people assumed that things had never been so bad for the dollar. At least they thought so until the onset of the 1995 currency crisis.

We do not have to go back to 1973, though, for an example of how an external shock can cause a dollar crisis. In late

December 1994, the collapse of the Mexican peso did exactly

that. And it is not totally outside of the realm of possibility that we could see a rerun of the "tequila effect." Mexico is by no means out of the woods. On May 25, 1995, for example, a rumor went around that, despite the $52 billion bailout package, Mexico might have to default on its *tesabonos*. This sent chills through the foreign exchange market and caused the dollar to drop 3 percent against the yen in a matter of a few hours. The rumor, of course, proved false. But it evoked yet another memory—that of August 1982, when Mexico did default on its massive foreign debt, bringing on the Latin American "debt crisis" that sent that entire region into a decade-long period of economic stagnation. Should the current Mexico recovery fail, and should Mexico be forced to default again, there can be little doubt that another major dollar crisis would follow.

What is most likely to cause the next currency crisis in America? It may arise for a very simple reason, with the sudden realization that what Professors Feldstein and Krugman have been telling us all along is true:

> Even if the United States now finally begins to move toward a balanced budget in the year 2002, this will result in a *weaker,* not a stronger dollar.

And as Dr. Cline and Dr. Bergsten have been saying:

> Even if the United States continues its trade war with Japan, it will not help either to balance America's overall trade deficit or to strengthen the dollar.

If and when the proof of this, in the form of statistical evidence, gradually surfaces, the key players in global financial markets would more or less simultaneously

- revise their views about the long-run equilibrium exchange rate
- demand a risk premium on U.S. assets

- see this as another pending "peso problem" and simply cut and run from the dollar before its next devaluation.

How likely is this to happen? And how soon might it start?

The Economist has an answer. In an article discussing America's national debt it suggested that, relatively speaking, the United States was in good shape: The ratio of net public sector debt to GDP in the United States was only 38 percent, as compared to 60 percent in Europe. So any worries that Washington would be unable to service its domestic debt, such as those that arose during the impasse on budget talks in late 1995 and early 1996, were totally misplaced. That was a phoney crisis. But the article went on to say:

> *Even without gazing so far into the future,* however, there is another reason why it is right to be worried about America's public finances. . . . the persistent current account deficits which over the past decade have transformed America from the world's biggest net foreign creditor into its largest debtor. . . . So long as this debt continues to mount, the dollar will remain vulnerable. *Here, one day, may lie a future real crisis in place of the present phoney one.*[5]

If *The Economist* is right about this real crisis arising not very far in the future, then the same "destructive" forces that we saw at work in the first half of 1995 would return to the scene. If the usual suspects, namely the Asian central banks, the hedge funds, the commercial banks, and the investment banks of the world, decide to marshal their forces and attack again in anticipation of another killing in the foreign exchange market, how far would the dollar fall this time? Put very crudely, the dollar would have to drop until it reached the point where it was generally accepted, even by the speculators and "rogue" central banks, that American exports had become so cheap, and imports had become so expensive, that it was now a sure thing that America's overall trade deficit would move back into balance.

But next time would the dollar make as soft a landing as it did in 1995, when after its exchange value hit lows of 79 yen and 1.34 deutsche marks it steadied and then gradually recovered to well over 100 yen and 1.50 deutsche marks? Not necessarily. Remember that this soft landing was not a product of free market forces. The key player in the global foreign exchange market in the second half of 1995 was, beyond any doubt, the Bank of Japan, which bought $100 billion dollars in order to boost its value in terms of yen. There are limits to how much further the Japanese central bank will be willing to go along this path, especially if market forces start to push the dollar down again and the huge amount of dollars that the Bank of Japan now owns—estimated at $250 billion—are worth less and less. If the "steadying force" of effective central bank intervention is absent next time, the foreign exchange markets could spin out of control.

This could very well leave a large financial institution— a key global player in all financial markets—holding the bag. Heretofore we have been talking about the recent spectacular successes of currency speculators, but there have been some spectacular failures as well. It is said that our old friend, George Soros, for example, *lost* $600 million when he was on the wrong side of the yen in January 1995, and Barings Brothers lost over a billion dollars when it bet the wrong way on the direction of Japanese interest rates and stock prices in 1995 and was forced into bankruptcy as a result. In addition, many large investment banks in both New York and London totally misjudged the direction of interest rates in early 1994 and lost many billions in the bond markets and on interest rates futures. They all survived. But in 1974 Bankhaus Herstatt of Cologne was not so lucky, forced to suddenly close its doors because of currency speculation that had gone terribly wrong. Despite the fact that it was not that big a bank and hardly a key player in the global banking system, it did have a large-scale foreign exchange business. Its closure | 71

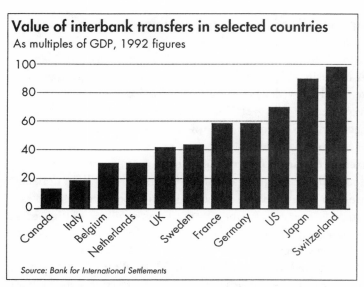

Value of interbank transfers in selected countries

As multiples of GDP, 1992 figures

Canada, Italy, Belgium, Netherlands, UK, Sweden, France, Germany, US, Japan, Switzerland

Source: Bank for International Settlements

Figure 7.5

took place after the settlement of the deutsche mark leg of foreign exchange transactions but before settlement of the dollar leg. In other words, the U.S. banks doing business with Herstatt did not get the dollars they were due after they had already paid the marks they owed the German bank. Some of Herstatt's trading partners, faced with nonpayment, then refused to make payments on their own account or for customers. The result was a chain reaction that, in essence, froze transfers between banks and brought the whole financial system to a halt, a result that subsequently became known as "the Herstatt effect."

At that time, the scale of interbank transfers were minuscule compared to what they are now. In Japan, for example, the value of transfers of funds jumped from 20 times national output to almost 100 times GDP in 1990. According to the Bank for International Settlements, it takes less than three business days for Japan's interbank funds transfer systems to generate turnover equivalent to the country's annual economic output. It takes just over three days in the United States and about four days in Germany. As Peter Norman pointed out in an article in the *Financial Times,* "Payments and Settlements," from which much of this discussion is derived, the increase in the demand for payments and settlement services reflects partly an expansion of domestic money market transactions in many countries, partly the ballooning of foreign exchange market turnover in line with globalization, and partly the rapid growth and internationalization of turnover in securities. The risks related to this "ballooning" of transactions are concentrated in the major international banks. Because of their payments role, such banks have been providing ever larger overdrafts to customers in the course of a day's business. Norman points out that:

> Big UK clearing banks have at times found the equivalent
> of their entire capital committed in temporary overdrafts by
> mid-morning. This need not matter if business flows nor-
> mally. But in event of a failure the authorities *could be*
> *confronted with a chain reaction that could jeopardise the*
> *world financial system.*

The Bank for International Settlements (BIS), an institution that hardly is given to scare tactics, says that "large and unpredictable exposures, together with limited information about their true size and distribution, make up the mixture which could spread and intensify financial shocks." The BIS then goes on to discuss possible financial meltdown with "distress sales of assets, leading to general price declines and undermining the solvency of institutions."

The problem related to "large and unpredictable expo-
sures together with limited information about their true size" does not just relate to forward foreign exchange positions of banks. Increasingly, it arises from a whole host of financial derivatives—such as "knockout options"—to which banks are parties. In fact, it is the banks themselves that increasingly operate outside formal futures exchanges and "customize"

derivative products designed to meet specific customer needs for hedging risks. Such proprietary trading involves the biggest names in global finance, but it is American financial institutions that lead the way. Why do they do it? As a leading banker in the Euromarkets puts it, with only mild exaggeration, 90 percent of the work of big investment banks is now unprofitable and serves only as a loss leader for highly profitable proprietary trading in derivatives. The value of outstanding contract amounts for American banks alone could now exceed $10,000,000,000,000,000.

The risks in the derivatives business are not restricted to financial institutions. Kashima Oil of Japan recently found that it had lost $1.4 billion in foreign exchange derivative trading. Germany's Metalgesellschaft, one of that country's oldest and most prestigious corporations, lost $1.4 billion in oil derivatives it was using to "hedge" its position in the American market and was forced to cut tens of thousands of jobs. As John Plender points out in his article "Through a market, darkly" in the *Financial Times*, "Hardly a week goes by without another expensive mishap in the use of derivatives—instruments such as swaps, futures and options whose value is 'derived' from more conventional financial assets."

Why so many mishaps carrying such huge price tags? The costs are related, of course, to the immense leverage available in derivatives trading, but that hardly explains so many "accidents." Many observers believe that too many of the men running both large corporations and large financial institutions simply do not understand derivatives and won't admit it either to others or to themselves. Then one fine day a 26-year old trader who works in the department responsible for the company's risk management walks into his office, eyes downcast, to tell him that there had been a slight accident. He had just lost quite a bit of money in "inverse floaters." The boss does not know an inverse floater from the smoke rising from his Partagas cigar. All he wants to know is how much. And when he is told that the loss equals the company's entire annual profit, as has already been pointed out in the case of Barings Bank where it was more then the bank's entire capital, it is the trader who gets fired, not he. Plender writes:

> The worry about derivatives lies less in the nature of the risks being run, than the wider context which is dangerously opaque. The Bank of England concluded last year that the unsupervised status of some of the large players in the system "does represent a supervisory hole at the very heart of the derivatives market." . . . Most central bankers claim that the probability that the mispricing of risks in derivatives could lead to a systemic shock is low, but cannot be ignored. They also worry that . . . complex derivative linkages across global markets could then make the contagion hard to contain.

"Contagion" is the key word here. Simulations carried out on the CHIPS system, one of the two large interbank transfer systems in the United States, have suggested that an unexpected failure by a big participant could result in nearly half of all institutions being unable to settle transactions, with perhaps a third of them being left in limbo. And because the dollar is the currency in which the vast majority of global financial transactions are settled, if the American clearing system goes down, so does the world's. The risk of a meltdown caused by an uncontrolled plunge in the dollar, which could set off a chain reaction that would start in the foreign exchange market but then spread throughout all derivative markets, is definitely there.

So how deeply concerned should we be, given that financial crashes inevitably affect the welfare of everyone? Governments, above all, are aware of this and should events appear to be getting out of control as a result of an unexpected severe plunge in the dollar, they could no longer just stand aside. As we have noted, during the 1995 crisis, intervention in the foreign exchange markets by the central banks of the Group of Ten was mostly notable for its absence. But should the dollar begin to drop again, the Bank of Japan and the Bundesbank— which, combined, accumulated well over $100 billion in the

Intervening Less Often

U.S. intervention in currency markets, 1989-1995

YEAR	TOTAL	FREQUENCY (# OF DAYS WITH INTER-VENTION)
1989	Sell $8.90 billion for marks Sell $10.58 billion for yen	97
1990	Sell $200 million for marks Sell $2.18 billion for yen	16
1991	Buy $1.34 billion for marks Sell $520 million for marks Sell $30 million for yen	13
1992	Buy $1.27 billion with marks Sell $250 million for yen	8
1993	Buy $1.43 billion with yen	5
1994	Buy $3.50 billion with marks Buy $2.60 billion with yen	5
1995	Buy $2.85 billion with marks* Buy $2.07 billion with yen	8**

* Through June
** Including three days in July and August

Note: Buying dollars (with yen or marks) tends to boost its value. Selling dollars (for yen or marks) tends to lower its value

Source: Federal Reserve

Figure 7.6 Source: *The Wall Street Journal,* September 14, 1995. Reprinted by permission of *The Wall Street Journal,* © 1995 Dow Jones & Company, Inc. All Rights Reserved Worldwide.

second half of 1995 in order to stabilize the dollar's value—would be faced with the need to buy huge amounts of dollars lest their currencies soar to unacceptable levels. But at this point, they might well say that enough is enough. They would, correctly, assert that it is the United States that has the ultimate responsibility for maintaining the integrity of the world's reserve currency, that it was no longer acceptable that the United States keep transferring the foreign exchange risk of holding dollars to other central banks. It would then be the Federal Reserve's and the U.S. Treasury's turn to assume that risk by issuing notes and bonds denominated in yen and marks and by using extensive swap agreements with foreign central banks under which they could borrow enough yen, marks, and francs to mop up tens of billions of U.S. dollars, if necessary, to prevent further price deterioration of the U.S. currency. As the preceding chart shows, despite the severity of the dollar crisis in 1995, U.S. intervention in the currency markets under the Clinton administration was actually less frequent than in prior years, and the amounts involved were insignificant.

Would this nonintervention policy of the United States be subject to change if another severe dollar crisis arose and foreign central banks refused to accumulate additional massive amounts of dollars? There can be little doubt that it would for the simple reason that the United States would act out of self-interest. It is one thing to use dollar devaluation and yen appreciation to solve America's trade deficit problem. It is quite another to allow the managers of the world's hedge funds to destroy the dollar and thus the credibility of the United States as a world power. Should such a crisis develop, the United States would act quickly and decisively. In fact, just the announcement of America's *intent* to do so would no doubt alleviate such a crisis. Assuming all of this transpired, those who are of the pessimistic school of thought believe the exchange rate would end up at 90 to 95 yen to the dollar, with the Swiss franc at 110 to the dollar and the mark at 1.35. What would be the economic and financial consequences of this?

For Japan, there can be no doubt that it would represent a new setback. It would result in a major, probably irrevocable, shrinkage of Japanese-based production of everything from vehicles to semiconductors. It would add another $100 billion foreign exchange loss to the immense losses that Japanese investors in dollar assets have already suffered. And what would happen to stock and real estate prices in Japan? In both areas, a rising yen has been associated with falling prices.

JAPANESE REAL ESTATE VALUES CONTINUE TO FALL

Index, 1990=100

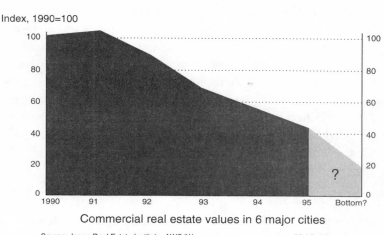

Commercial real estate values in 6 major cities

Source: Japan Real Estate Institute, AWSJW   Nichibei Associates

Figure 7.7

     The trend in golf course membership prices, which historically has been a good predictor of land price trends, suggests that even without new yen appreciation, land prices are likely to remain weak, despite the fact that the Nikkei's nation-wide golf course membership index is in 1996 down 75 percent below peak levels. This reflects not just an oversupply of buildings, especially of commercial office space, but more importantly a consensus on Japan's economic growth prospects. Land prices in Japan outpaced GNP during the growth era of the 1960s and early 1970s, but they moved back in line with GNP in the late 1970s and early 1980s. But in the first half of 1995, as Japan moved into a period of negative growth, land prices plummeted, falling 13.1 percent in Japan's six major cities, the steepest six-month drop on record, reflecting how bearish Japan's future GNP growth was being viewed. Since then, even though the yen moved to well over 100 to the dollar, and the economy began to recover, land prices have continued to slide.

If, however, the yen moves back into the 90 to 95 yen to the dollar range, it stands to reason that this will make the consensus view of Japanese growth prospects once again bearish. The effect on real estate prices will be exactly the same as it has been before: They will decline even further. This possibility of a further decline, though, is obviously dependent upon whether or not real estate prices in Japan have already plummeted as far as they possibly can as well as upon whether or not a rebound is in sight.

Where the stock market is concerned, the same general thinking would appear to apply: The higher the yen, the lower the stock market. But the same reservation applies here as applies to real estate, namely whether or not the stock market has already discounted the possibility of the yen moving back to a higher level, inducing a corresponding lower rate of future economic growth. What would seem to be a safe assumption is that if the yen does move back into the 90 to 95 range and stays there, the rally in the Japanese stock market which took it well above the 20,000 level would fizzle. However, should the yen settle in well above 100, profits of Japanese multinational corporations and banks would rise, and the 1996 Nikkei bull market would continue.

For the United States, the consequences are seemingly more difficult to forecast. When the dollar crashed in 1995, both the stock and the bond markets went the other way. The next time, though, it may well be quite different. When asked what might upset American securities markets in the future, one of the most astute observers of these markets, Henry Kaufman, who is otherwise very optimistic, answered that the only event that would cause deep concern would be a further "crumbling" of the dollar.

What would be the basis for such concern? Initially, it would be the portfolio diversification that would take place if the dollar begins to sink again—primarily sales of U.S. bonds by foreign investors. Japanese life insurance companies would be of strategic importance in this process, since they have been the largest private foreign investors in U.S. government notes and

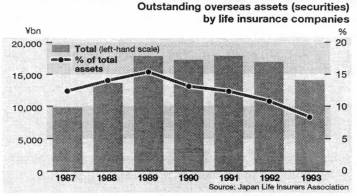

Figure 7.8 Source: Gerard Baker, "Stay-at-Home Investors Drive the Yen's Rise: The Foreign Assets of Japan's Giant Financial Institutions Have Been Falling Fast, *The Financial Times,* April 21, 1995, p. 5. Reprinted by permission of *The Financial Times* © 1995. All Rights Reserved Worldwide.

bonds as well as other dollar-denominated securities, holding total assets of ¥150,000 billion, an amount equal to one-third of Japanese GDP. These companies led the recycling of Japan's current account surplus in the 1980s, accounting for almost 60 percent of Japan's capital outflows during that decade, according to the *Financial Times*'s Gerard Baker. For the past five years, however, they have been in full retreat.

Although such a retreat from the U.S. bond market would normally have put downward pressure on bond prices, simultaneous buying of U.S. government securities by foreign central banks more than compensated for private divestment. If, however, those central banks balk at assuming more foreign exchange risks the next time, the end result will be quite different. Investors, such as those Japanese life insurance companies, will now demand a major risk premium where the yields on dollar bonds are concerned, without which their gradual exodus from dollar bonds would turn into a flight. What would develop, as bond yields soared, would be an acutely inverse yield curve, and that, as most investors know, is historically a precursor to recession. If this scenario plays itself out and bond prices rise sharply, the anticipation of the consequences for future economic growth and corporate profits in the United States would send stocks sharply lower. This time it would be the American bubble that would burst.

This, then, is what *could* happen in another currency crisis. In both the United States and Japan securities markets would be badly damaged, economic growth would be temporarily stopped, and unemployment would rise. And finally, in the United States, fears would arise, justified or not, that import prices would spike as a result of the collapsed dollar, resulting in the worst of all worlds: stagflation.

All of this would hardly be looked upon with indifference by other countries. After all, the United States and Japan are two of the three engines of growth that pull along the rest of the world. If Japan's economic growth was again stifled by a new rise in the yen, the most affected would be those booming nations of Southeast Asia that depend on Japanese consumer demand for their exports and capital from Japanese banks for their development. Both would be seriously impaired.

Japan's banks, which since 1990 have been reeling from the effects of the bursting of the two domestic bubbles, would see the value of their collateral and securities holdings decline still further, meaning that their *overall* capacity and willingness to lend would be reduced. The reluctance to lend abroad would be even more pronounced, applying even to loans denominated in yen. The banks' retreat from foreign exposure would parallel that of the insurance companies.

Those areas that are most dependent on the United States for both trade and capital would likewise be victims of the fallout from the scenario described above. Chief among these would be the nations of the Western Hemisphere—from Canada to Mexico to Brazil—which depend heavily on exports to the United States as the most vibrant and open market for their products. If the American economy sinks into recession, or worse, extended stagnation resulting from the shock of a dollar collapse, that market will no longer be able to absorb all their planned exports, exports that they had relied upon to supply the foreign exchange needed to fuel their domestic economic growth. The shrinkage of their export potential could be further exacerbated by the fact that their goods, as all foreign goods, would then become very expensive as a result of further dollar devaluation, opening the way for substitution by similar products produced in the United States. As their foreign exchange earnings shrank, so would their ability to attract foreign investment capital. Any foreign lender must look first and foremost at a country's ability to service its external loans and repay them on maturity. Healthy foreign exchange reserves are key to fulfilling that requirement. When a country's trade balance suddenly turns negative—be it because of rapidly rising imports, as was the case of Mexico in 1994, or as a result of rapidly falling exports, as with the shrinkage of demand in its primary export market—the inflow of capital turns into an exodus.

Europe would hardly remain immune to this problem. It is not just that the American market is of strategic importance for the German automobile industry or for the French fashion industry, or that the Japanese market for Swedish timber or Swiss watches is integral to those countries. Rather, should both the United States and Japan go into sudden eclipse simultaneously, the entire global trade in everything from oil to diamonds to shoes would begin to shrink. It would be a process that could result in *global* deflation, about the last thing Europe can afford with average unemployment near 12 percent.

How close are we to such speculations about the future becoming reality? Let's put it another way: Even in the absence of a major crisis triggered by the collapse of the dollar, are both Japan and the United States facing an inevitable eclipse of their economic power?

Part III

8

THERE WERE—and are—those who believe that Japan and the United States are indeed facing an inevitable eclipse of their economic power.

Let's begin with the United States. At the beginning of the 1990s, the conventional wisdom was that the United States was entering a period of irreversible economic decline in both absolute and relative terms. Americans were told that the standard of living of future generations would never again top that of the post–World War II generation. They were assured that in the 1990s the United States would be relegated to Number Three, behind both Japan and a Europe led by Germany. They were warned that America's banking system was on the verge of collapse. They were given to believe that the dollar was finished as the currency of choice around the world, soon to be replaced by the ecu (the European Currency Unit) and the yen, and that their country's technological lead in such key areas as semiconductors had vanished forever. They were warned that the Big Three automobile manufacturers based in Detroit were so far behind the rest of the world in terms of technology and design that by the end of the decade it would be a wonder if even one of them survived. To make matters even worse, Americans were informed that their educational system had deteriorated to such a degree that a turnaround in any of these areas was impossible.

These "truths" were hammered home from all sides by experts and pseudoexperts alike. Michael Crichton, a medical doctor by training, in his novel *Rising Sun* (1991), assured American readers that the Japanese were out to bury the United States, and due to their wicked cunning and deviousness, they would succeed. The fact that four years later Japan was in recession, its government in disarray, its competitive stature in the world seriously undermined by the sky-high exchange value of the yen, and under attack by the United States on the issue of trade, does not deter many from still believing the warnings of the novel. Even the *New York Times Book Review* hailed Crichton as "America's Most Serious Suspense Novelist."

MIT economist Lester Thurow, who normally deserves to be taken more seriously, told Americans in his book *Head to Head: The Coming Economic Battle Among Japan, Europe and America* that it would not be the Japanese but the Germans who were destined to become the new power relegating the United States to the status of second-best, or worse, long before this decade was over. Two years after this prediction, Germany experienced its worst economic crisis since World War II, pulling all of Europe down with it, as the German unemployment rate headed toward 12 percent.

The Yale historian Paul Kennedy took a grander view of America's future in his book, *The Rise and Fall of the Great Powers,* but his conclusion was the same. Kennedy sounded a very pessimistic note for the future of the United States, gaining a great deal of credence, especially in academic circles, both in the United States and abroad. Kennedy's historical analysis of the fate of superpowers through the ages led him to conclude that America was losing its status as a globally dominant power and that the twentieth century would be its one and only century to shine. He sought to convince Americans that the permanent eclipse of the power of the United States would be just the latest in a series of great power collapses during the past four centuries caused in all cases by global overreach relative to a superpower's economic base.

It is fair to say that, except for the decline of the dollar, all of these dire predictions have been wrong. In fact, it is America that is in ascendancy once again, while it is Europe and Japan that have faltered. It is Americans who finally recognized who the real enemy was: the profligate, complacent America of the 1980s. The response was drastic: During the first half of the 1990s corporate America restructured itself on all levels, from the board room to the factory floor. To be sure, this process was given a tremendous boost when the Berlin Wall came down in 1989 and the Cold War came to an end, for this meant that although the Soviet Union had literally spent itself to death on armaments, this same process could be reversed where the United States was concerned. America could now concentrate on mending itself at home, rather than on preparing to fight the Soviet Union. This realization is very important, since it puts a dagger right through the heart of Professor Kennedy's forecast of the "fall" of the United States as a superpower.

Kennedy's thesis was that great power eclipses are always caused by global military overstretch relative to a superpower's domestic economic base. This is precisely what *did* happen to the former Soviet Union, so Kennedy was at least half right. But where the United States is concerned, he was dead wrong. As a result of America's winning the Cold War, the burden of protecting the free world, which it had borne almost singlehandedly since 1947, was gradually lifted. The demise of the Soviet Union meant that the United States could safely embark upon the demilitarization of the American economy, a process that is already beginning to alter the economic future of the United States. For example, at the end of the 1980s, $185 billion of America's $300 billion defense budget was devoted to preparing to fight Russia in a European land war. Most of its $30 billion intelligence budget was devoted to the same end. The projected spending of $120 billion on a scientifically useless space station as a symbol of America's leadership in space was in the same category. All such expenditures are now in the process of being drastically cut. Add to the list military base closings, the drastic reduction of weapons procurement, from nuclear submarines to B-2 bombers, and cuts in the size of its armed forces (almost half before the end of the decade). All of these resources which have been "squandered" during the past four-and-a-half decades can now be redeployed in the private sector, devoted to | 8 7 making butter not guns. To be sure, had the United States not "armed the Soviet Union to death" all of this would never have been possible—so the use of the word "squander" is used only in a purely economic context. But all that is now history. So much for the global military overstretch which was going to bring down the United States and bring it down irrevocably.

What has happened in the private sector of the United States during the first half of the 1990s is no less dramatic. To describe what has occurred, one must hearken back to the teachings of one of the greatest economists of our century, Joseph Schumpeter. Schumpeter was a failed Austrian finance minister, which qualified him for a teaching job at Harvard, where he came up with the theory of "creative destruction." Put simply, his theory was that periodic gale force winds of change blow through the capitalistic system, blowing over what were considered the pillars of our capitalistic society. Out of the ashes of such destruction, propelled by technological innovation, venture capital, and entrepreneurship, rise phoenixes, which then lead society, through ever higher productivity, to new economic heights. During the past five years, the United States has been going through just such a process.

For example, when IBM's mainframe was brought down by the young hotshots at Sun and Apple, the computer company had to remake itself or face irrevocable decline. After restructuring, and firing 100,000 people in the process, it is now on the rise under new leadership. It's stock, which just a few years ago had sunk to $40, moved back to $100, showing that investors have recognized that the "new" IBM has the same growth and profit potential as the "old" IBM that almost went the way of the dinosaurs. Sears is another example. It too had to drastically change its ways when challenged by Wal-Mart's new marketing techniques. It rose to the challenge, although 50,000 workers and its CEO lost their jobs in the process. Sears is now back in the black. Chrysler was brought to the edge of extinction by Japanese competition. After drastically trimming costs and embarking on a make-or-break redesign program, Chrysler is now more profitable than ever before in its history, and its Jeep Cherokees are even selling well in Japan. The fact is that America has remade itself once again, as so often in the past, and the process is almost complete. As a result the United States now enjoys the highest rate of productivity on earth and the highest rates of productivity increases in a generation. This rising productivity is the key to the country's rising national prosperity and global competitive stature.

The dollar played a significant role in all this. It was the meteoric rise and fall of the dollar in the 1980s that brought to light how fat and complacent American industry had become. Moreover, it was thought that when America's trade deficit ballooned from $26 billion in 1980 to $159 billion in 1987 it was all due to the overvaluation of the dollar. As Harvard economist Benjamin Friedman put it in his book, *Day of Reckoning,* "It is difficult to escape the conclusion that the 74% average *increase* in dollar exchange rates between 1980 and 1985 . . . was the greatest single factor eroding the competitiveness of our industry."[1] Friedman concluded, "With a lower dollar, American industries will once again be able to compete effectively." To be sure, this proved true for the next four years, but then the deficits began to balloon again, ultimately reaching record heights. The cause was not domestic inflation, which had been brought under control, so the basic reason for America's loss of competitiveness had to lie elsewhere. Americans then realized that the enemy was ourselves, not the dollar and not inflation. So with the excuses gone, America finally began to knuckle down and restructure itself from top to bottom. *This realization and restructuring is of fundamental importance for the future of the dollar.*

Michael Prowse, writing "A strategy for dollar revival" for the *Financial Times,* summed up why.

> The strongest plus for the dollar is the vitality of US industry. After painful restructuring in the past decade, corporate America is arguably in better shape than at any

time since the 1950s. Capital spending has contributed more to this upturn than to any in recent memory. Non-residential fixed investment has risen by 40 per cent in real terms since early 1991. Profits have soared. And exporters have regained market share in many sectors. . . .

Given this underlying industrial strength, quite modest policy adjustments would probably be sufficient to alter decisively sentiment towards the dollar.

What kind of "quite modest policy adjustments" are necessary? And are they already underway? First and foremost, Prowse writes, "would be to tackle the root cause of dollar weakness: low national savings." The shortest route to that goal is a significant reduction of dissavings in the form of America's budget deficit. That process is well underway, in an almost miraculous fashion. Two years ago no one would have thought that there would be any serious effort even to attempt to balance the budget in our generation, and yet in 1996 there was a consensus among both Democrats and Republicans to balance the budget by the year 2002. To be sure, as we have already noted, it is the opinion of some of America's leading economists that as a result of this process, the dollar will sink and the U.S. trade deficit will rise in the near term. But if America gets through this danger zone without the worst (as described in Part II of this book) actually happening, the dollar crisis of 1995 will be just a bad memory before this decade is over. With national savings moving back up toward acceptable levels, the "root cause" of the decline will lose its force.

The second way for America to renew confidence in the dollar would be to send a clear signal that Washington cares about the dollar. This would mean an abandonment of any further hint of either benign neglect or further competitive devaluation. As Judy Shelton points out in her book *Money Meltdown,* Americans tend to have a naive or even blasé attitude about the dollar relative to other currencies, an attitude that, at least for a while, seemed to extend to the very top level of the

Clinton administration. This goes far in explaining why U.S. Treasury Secretary Lloyd Bentsen made it known in February 1993 that he "would like to see a higher yen." As Shelton points out, as the weeks went by, it increasingly began to look as if Bentsen's comment was no off-the-cuff quip but rather part of a purposeful strategy. She goes on to say:

> If the exchange markets needed confirmation that the Clinton administration wanted a weak dollar to reduce the U.S. trade deficit with Japan, they received it when President Clinton voiced his own satisfaction that the sliding dollar-yen rate was turning out to be an effective tool of U.S. trade policy, one of the things that in his words was "working."[2]

The day before Bentsen's remark, the yen was trading at the rate of 119.15 to the dollar. Four months later, the dollar hit a postwar low of 104.80; two years later it had collapsed to under 80. During the first half of the Clinton administration, then, the dollar lost one-third of its value against the yen.

As Christopher Wood points out in his book *The End of Japan, Inc.,* the bureaucrats at the top of Japan's Ministry of Finance completely misjudged the Clinton administration. They thought that it was staffed with pragmatists who would recognize the differences between the Japanese and American perceptions of capitalism and not try to force change, unlike Clinton's Republican, ideology-driven predecessors. They were wrong. "For the people in America who argue that Japan is different," writes Woods, "are precisely those who call for taking the toughest economic sanctions against Japan in terms of managed trade or even outright protection."[3] He could have added competitive devaluation to the list.

Finally, on the last day of May 1995, the U.S. government seemed to realize that any continuation of the policy of competitive devaluation could lead to very serious trouble. So for the first time since the start of the 1995 currency crisis, the U.S. Treasury (and some of its G-7 partners) finally stepped in, selling an estimated $5 billion of yen and marks for dollars. It worked. The dollar, which had again begun to fade as a result of Mickey Kantor's trade confrontation with Japan, snapped back by two yen and three pfennig. Then the Bank of Japan stepped in, buying $100 billion during the second half of 1995 and pushing the exchange value of the dollar to well over 100 yen. The chief spokesman of the U.S. Treasury, Deputy Secretary Lawrence Summers, also changed his tune, repeatedly expressing satisfaction with the falling yen and rising dollar, indicating that both countries could live with a yen/dollar exchange value of 100. This was very encouraging for businessmen and government alike, both of whom much prefer a stable dollar and yen to the chaotic gyrations that both currencies had been going through in recent times. Were the United States now consistently to follow through, even to the point of hinting at its willingness to using the ultimate weapon in its currency stabilization arsenal, namely the issue of Treasury notes and bonds denominated in yen and marks, then the second pillar of support for the dollar would be in place.

What one *cannot* expect to happen is that the Federal Reserve will raise short-term interest rates in order to entice foreign capital, and thus prop up the dollar even further. This "classic" approach to currency problems is not an option because the American economy is again in a very delicate phase in the business cycle. If the Fed were to begin to raise rates significantly through progressive monetary tightening, it would most probably dump the United States into recession, and the Fed simply cannot allow that to happen. Neither can President Clinton. As *The Economist* has pointed out, recent history suggests that an incumbent president's chances of reelection depend on how the economy is doing. "The rule of thumb since the second world war is that growth of about 4 percent-plus in the four quarters leading up to the election will keep an incumbent in the White House; less than that, and he is in deep trouble."

So the "interest rate weapon" will remain unused in the

arsenal. But perhaps another factor—temporary slowing—will

help the United States bridge that "danger zone" for the dollar and allow it to arrive on very firm ground on the other side. Temporary slowing of the U.S. economy, as part of a normal business cycle, will result in lower imports and thus help both the trade deficit and the dollar.

But the news may be even better on the export side of the equation. U.S. exports are rising at rates seldom seen before, representing one of the strongest components of the American economy. In a recent study, the Geneva-based World Trade Forum polled the chief executives of 500 of the world's largest corporations asking their views on which countries were most competitive in the global marketplace. They ranked United States first, Singapore second, Hong Kong third, Japan fourth, Switzerland fifth, and Germany sixth. What determined these rankings? The partial answer lies with relative labor costs. The German magazine *Der Spiegel* conducted a study comparing current labor costs in Germany with those of its two chief competitors in the world economy, the United States, and Japan, with deutsch marks per hour as the unit of measurement. The United States ranked lowest by far, with an average of DM 28 per hour. Japan came in at DM 36 per hour, while Germany ranked by far the most expensive at DM 44 an hour. These results reflect a radical shift in the past decade. Just ten years ago, American wages were 35 percent higher than those in Germany; now they are 35 percent lower.

Wages alone do not, of course, determine how competitive a nation is—otherwise Haiti would be the most prosperous nation in the Western Hemisphere—something neither Ross Perot nor Pat Buchanan seem to comprehend. Rather, labor costs are only meaningful when combined with labor productivity. Here again we find the United States on top. A study done by McKinsey, MIT, and the University of Groeningen concluded that the average American worker produced $50,000 per year in goods and services, while the average German worker produced only $44,000. Their Japanese counterpart produced just $37,000 of output per person year.

But what about the collapse of the dollar? Could it not seriously undermine America's future competitive stature? Doesn't classic economic theory teach that what always follows such a currency collapse is a substantial increase in the rate of domestic inflation? This theory certainly does not appear to apply to the United States. One obvious reason for this is that imports still play a relatively small role in the overall economy— just 12 percent of GDP. Moreover, some of America's major imports are commodities that are globally priced in dollars. Chief among these is crude oil. Whether the dollar moves from 105 to the yen to 95 doesn't affect the American cost of imported oil: It was $20 a barrel a couple of years ago, and it is in the range of $20 a barrel today. A third very important factor is the high degree of competition in the American market, the most open market in the world, where domestic and foreign producers, playing on a level field, have to fight it out for market share like nowhere else on earth. The Japanese and European car manufacturers have learned this the hard way. As the dollar fell against their currencies, meaning that what they now got per vehicle in either yen or marks was substantially less than before, they could not raise their dollar prices and thus solve their problem at the expense of the American consumer, pushing up the rate of American inflation in the process. For the most part, due to the fact that Detroit was now producing competing models very similar in quality to imports and often lower in price, foreign producers had to absorb the difference or lose market share. So their profits went down instead of the American rate of inflation going up.

The numbers bear this out. In the 12 months ending April 30, 1995—a period during which the most significant decline in the value of the dollar occurred—U.S. import prices (such as that of oil) increased just 4.7 percent, as compared to a 3.1 percent increase in the overall consumer price index during the same period. (And again, imports account for only 12 percent of the goods and services bought in America.) Even if you calculate in a 12-month lag between the dollar devaluation and its effect on prices, the conclusion remains the same. The rate of inflation in 1996 as measured by the Consumer Price Index (CPI) will most probably barely exceed the 2.8 percent rate of 1995. There are those, including Alan Greenspan, that are convinced that the CPI overstates the real rate of inflation by as much as a full percentage point. If so, the U.S. rate would be nearly in line with the rates of inflation in both Germany and Japan. Given all this, plus the fact that the American economy is slowing to a rate of growth that is compatible with continuing relative price stability, there is no danger that inflation is going to undermine the future of the American economy.

One could summarize the current outlook for the U.S. economy as follows:

- a 2.0 percent growth in 1996, rising to 2.5 percent in 1997;
- a 3 percent rate of (unadjusted) inflation in 1996 and 1997;
- a 5.75 percent rate of unemployment.

Looking beyond this, it seems highly likely that the secular trend in the United States is upward for the remainder of the 1990s. What is currently happening in northern California exemplifies what is happening in the United States in general and why.

At the end of the 1980s, California was hit very hard by a double whammy. The first punch was a recession, which caused the California real estate bubble to burst. This resulted in massive unemployment in the construction industry and the real estate business in general, an industry that has always been a key segment of the California economy. The second blow was the structural change in the California economy necessitated by the end of the Cold War and the resulting implosion of the huge defense-related sector of the California economy. The effects were widespread and devastating: Tens of thousands of employees of aerospace manufacturers as well as entire communities dependent upon the presence of military bases were out of work.

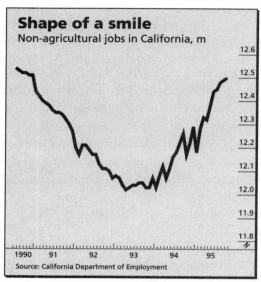

Figure 8.1   Source: *The Economist,* December 2, 1995. © 1995 The Economist Newspaper Group, Inc. Reprinted with permission. Further reproduction prohibited.

The state lost over 600,000 jobs within a very short time, and it was said that the California dream was over.

But these predictions are proving to be as wrong as those of Thurow and Kennedy. Look at the comeback in California employment.

What has happened is that California is remaking itself along Schumpeterian lines. New, high-quality jobs by the tens of thousands are again being created. The model is the San Francisco Bay area, where world-class scientists and engineers are being trained by the thousands at Stanford University and the University of California at Berkeley. What is often overlooked is that these universities attract not only the best brains in California and many other parts of the United States but also scholars from literally every nation on earth. A very high percentage of these scholars stay in the United States after completing their studies, adding to the country's elite "brain pool." Thus 40 percent of the Nobel Prizes that have come to the United States were earned by men and women who were born abroad. This "open door" policy that brings so many intellectuals to the United States is often overlooked by those who predict the decline of America due to the gross inadequacies of its school systems. While it's true that its public primary and secondary schools are inadequate as measured by any historic or international standard, its universities, especially its graduate schools, are unmatched anywhere on earth.

Besides scientists and engineers, the Bay Area also breeds entrepreneurs by the thousands, most of them coming out of Silicon Valley. The model is, of course, that of Steve Wozniak and Steve Jobs, two young men who walked out of Hewlett Packard, set up their own operation in a garage near Palo Alto, and there gave birth to Apple Computer. The area in which such entrepreneurial energy is most visible today is computer software, an industry on which the United States has a lock, light years ahead of both Europe and Asia. The largest cluster of key players in this industry is around San Francisco.

But no entrepreneur can develop and bring his technological innovations to fruition and market without capital, especially venture capital. Again, it is in San Francisco where one can find one of the biggest clusters of venture capitalists on earth. Such names as Hambrecht and Quist or Montgomery Securities are synonymous with capital that is both high-tech and risk-oriented. Marry these three elements and you have exactly what Schumpeter prescribed: economic growth propelled by technological innovation, venture capital, and entrepreneurship.

The Bay Area is also the world capital of biotechnology. As one observer has put it, the military industrial complex begat Silicon Valley, which begat a new breed of high-tech entrepreneurs, who begat the biotech industry. Today there are 350 biotech companies in the United States, the majority of them in the Bay Area, as compared to 150 such companies in Europe and less than 100 in Japan. As a result, major *foreign* pharmaceutical companies have little choice but to come to California to get a piece of the action lest they be left in the dust. Thus the largest pharmaceutical company in the world based on stock market capitalization, Swiss-based Hoffmann La Roche, invested billions of dollars in the Bay Area's Genentech, essentially to fund research. Another Swiss pharmaceutical company, Ciba-Geigy, put more than a billion dollars in another Bay Area biotech company, Chiron, for the same reason, and later bought outright yet a third company, Syntex, for over $5 billion. Ciba-Geigy— now merged with Sandoz, another Swiss pharmaceutical giant, into a new company, Novartis—is also establishing its own independent biotech research facility in Palo Alto, right next to Stanford University.

Although the Bay Area is a model for the return of vibrancy to the American economy, the same sort of dynamism can be found in and around Boston; Austin, Texas; and even Detroit, where the American automobile industry has made a spectacular comeback in terms of everything from the quality of its vehicles to its unprecedented profits. Nevertheless, even technological innovation and entrepreneurship cannot get a nation back on top if the political framework in which they must operate is nonsupportive. Here too, the omens look good for America.

The Republican takeover of the House and Senate of the United States, and the rise of Newt Gingrich and his Contract with America in 1994 triggered a process that will change the role of government in America to one that is less intrusive and less expensive. Now both Republicans and Democrats agree on the need for welfare reform as well as a balanced budget in 2002. This means that we will see a gradual reversal of a 60-year trend that has led to ever larger and more intrusive government in the United States, which, in turn, has led Americans ever deeper into a welfare state. The reversal of this trend can only augur well for America's economic future.

So many other countries have learned this lesson the hard way when they allowed their governments to take over too large a proportion of the economy, with the result that everybody ended up losers. This was all too obvious where the former

Marxist states of Eastern Europe were concerned. There they

went all the way with state control, and in the end they also went all the way down the drain. But even the Swedish model—which so many had hoped would be a viable, more humane "third way"—has shown signs of disintegration. There the public sector grew until it represented over 60 percent of the Swedish economy, with the result that Sweden has fallen from second to fourteenth in the world in terms of per capita GDP in 20 years and is still falling. That fate surely will not befall America.

There is also a new—although quite different—factor at work that also augurs well for the United States, namely its leadership role in moving toward a Western Hemisphere common market. The first step in this direction was, of course, the creation of the North American Free Trade Agreement (NAFTA) in 1993, which brought down all trade barriers between the United States, Canada, and Mexico. In December 1994, at a conference in Miami that included every head of state in the Western Hemisphere except Fidel Castro, President Clinton pledged to extend this common market to the entire Western Hemisphere. This will be done progressively, with Chile probably the next country to enter.

On January 1, 1995, another significant event occurred: the creation of the brand new Southern Common Market embracing Argentina, Brazil, Uruguay, and Paraguay, which makes virtually all trade between these countries duty free. When the Southern Common Market, which will soon embrace all of South America, links up with NAFTA, the Free Trade Area of the Americas that will result will embrace 800 million consumers and represent a market of $12 trillion, far and away the largest market on earth. The target date for its creation is the year 2005. The Free Trade Area of the Americas will do for the Western Hemisphere what the creation of Common Market, following the signing of the Treaty of Rome in 1957, did for Europe, namely spur extra-proportional increases in cross-border trade among its member nations, resulting in higher rates of economic growth throughout the region. This growth effect is, after all, the primary reason for creating common markets. The aggregation

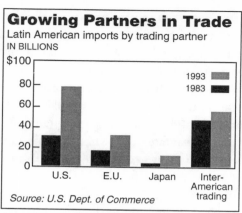

Growing Partners in Trade

Latin American imports by trading partner
IN BILLIONS

1993
1983

Source: U.S. Dept. of Commerce

Figure 8.2 Source: Thomas F. McClarty, III, "Hemispheric Free Trade is Still a National Priority," *The Wall Street Journal,* May 26, 1995, p. A11. Reprinted by permission of *The Wall Street Journal,* © 1995 Dow Jones & Company, Inc. All Rights Reserved Worldwide.

of markets results in ever greater economies of scale and ever sharper competition, an ongoing process that results in an upward shift in the rate of real economic growth. What happened in Europe after 1957 provides irrefutable historical evidence that the higher rate of growth could prevail for a decade or longer. There is, however, a big difference between Europe and the Americas, in that all these benefits lie ahead for the Western Hemisphere, whereas economic integration is more or less a spent force for Europe. Latin America is thus destined to play an important role in the economic future of the United States and has begun to do so today.

But what about tomorrow? After the Mexican fiasco, and the "tequila effect" that followed, how solid are Latin America's growth prospects for the rest of this decade? Will it prosper and remain a prime and growing market for American products, or will it falter and become a financial millstone around the neck of the United States?

Let's begin with Mexico. Mexico's excessive imports caused a huge trade deficit to develop, which led to expanding foreign debt and diminishing foreign exchange reserves, which resulted in turn in the peso crisis and the "tequila effect." The peso devaluation and the austerity programs that have been put into effect by the new Mexican government have already turned the situation around as far as the trade deficit, which is now in surplus, is concerned. As a result of the drastically lower peso/dollar exchange rate, Mexican exports are booming like never before, while imports of now very expensive foreign goods have dropped off precipitously. The rate of inflation is coming back under control, interest rates continue to fall, and even the stock market in Mexico City has recovered to record levels, at least in peso terms. Despite all this, the country remains in recession, unemployment is extremely high, and social unrest is growing. Reestablishing Mexico's health to where it was prior to the currency crisis is proving to be long and arduous, but by 1997 Mexico will probably be back on solid ground. When this happens, it will eliminate a potential "external shock" that might have precipitated another dollar crisis and brought this entire rosy scenario regarding America's economic future crashing down.

In the rest of Latin America, two countries—Brazil and Argentina—are of pivotal importance. Both nations now have remarkably low rates of inflation by historical standards as well as strong foreign exchange reserves. Moreover, gradual introduction of the new Southern Common Market will open up trade throughout all of Latin America. Although foreign investors are still wary after what happened in 1995 following the peso devaluation, they are beginning to return, since the long-term rewards promise to greatly outweigh the short-term risks. As Thomas McClarty, the Special Representative of the President and the Secretary of State for the Summit of the Americas, recently pointed out in the *Wall Street Journal,* "Latin America is growing so fast that its infrastructure alone will require an estimated $500 billion in investment in the coming decade."[4] Of prime importance for the economic future of both countries is their leadership. Both Brazilian president Fernando Henrique Cardosa and Argentine president Carlos Menem have superb credentials. Both are pro-democracy and pro–free market, and both enjoy crucial popular support. The World Bank estimates that the growth rate in all of Latin America will accelerate to over 6 percent between 1998 and 2005. So the future looks better than it ever has where the major trading partners of the United States in the southern half of the Western Hemisphere are concerned.

The various regional free trade arrangements that have been discussed all promise to bring positive benefits. But recently another proposal for a further expansion of such free trade zones has come up with less positive overtones. This is the suggestion being floated by the Atlanticists in both the American and European foreign policy establishments (including Foreign Minister Klaus Kinkel of Germany, former Foreign Secretary Douglas Hurd of Great Britain, and Sir Leon Brittan, vice president of the European Union's executive commission): to seek the creation of a Transatlantic Free Trade Agreement (TAFTA). This group has been joined by U.S. Secretary of State Warren Christopher, who said that the United States would seriously study the proposal because it has significant potential to promote growth on both sides of the Atlantic.

On the surface, this looks like yet another win-win proposal. But this ignores the nature of America's proposed partner in such an arrangement. It is not the governments of Germany or France that would be the partners of Washington, Ottawa, and Mexico City, but rather the Commission of the European Union, an executive body run by a very large, independent, and overpaid group of international bureaucrats, many of whom have very strong protectionist tendencies. This arouses the suspicion that their proposal is aimed more at joining forces with America in order to more effectively protect their markets from Japanese and Asian competition than at expanding internal trade and thus promoting economic growth.

The creation of common markets cuts two ways. As the two seminal thinkers on this subject, Professors Jacob Viner and

James Meade, pointed out early on, the joining of nations

within the framework of a customs union with free internal trade but common barriers to imports from third countries, such as tariffs or quotas, results in both trade creation and trade diversion. Meade, in *Problems of Economic Union,* explained it this way:

> The formation of a regional union may improve the economic use of world resources in so far as it "creates" trade by enabling one member of the union to undercut the uneconomic industries of another member, whereas it may worsen the use of the world's resources in so far as it "diverts" trade by inducing one member of the union to purchase the products of uneconomic industries in another preferentially favored member state rather than the products of the more economic industries of outsiders.[5]

European purchases of VCRs a number of years ago provide a good example of how this works. Japanese VCRs were vastly superior to anything made in Europe in terms of both quality and price. They were so competitive that even the common tariff surrounding the EC could not keep them out. So what did the French do? They assigned the import clearance of VCRs coming from Japan to an obscure, tiny customs office that was able to clear only a maximum of a few hundred units a week. So the French consumer had no choice but to continue to buy inferior, French-made VCRs. The Italians used similar tactics to keep out Japanese-made cars. The Commission in Brussels did nothing to stop this.

The most egregious protectionism practiced by the EU occurs in the agricultural sector. The vast majority of the EU's enormous budget goes to agricultural subsidies to support an inefficient agriculture sector that simply could not compete with American agribusiness if America farmers were given free access to European markets. This stands in contrast to the current situation in the United States, where a movement is underway to gradually eliminate farm subsidies due to lack of need. These different approaches to agriculture represent a fundamental incompatibility between the EU and the United States, an incompatibility that exists to a much greater degree between NAFTA and the EU. NAFTA is run by an extremely small secretariat with no sovereign power whatsoever. By contrast, the Commission of the EU has not only many sovereign powers in trade matters, but for decades it has managed to extend its sovereignty to many other areas, ranging from antitrust enforcement to the (protectionist) establishment of national standards. Now that the "growth effect" of the creation of the European Common Market is more or less exhausted, what is now emanating from Brussels probably results more in harmful trade diversion than it does in positive trade creation.

There is yet another reason for Americans to view the proposals for TAFTA with great suspicion, namely they ignore the historical imperative that the United States should shift from an Atlantic-oriented to a Pacific-oriented nation. That future is reflected in the industrial growth of Northern California as well as in the fact that Japan is now California's top trading partner, buying over $13 billion a year of the state's output of everything from computers to rice, to cotton, to movies. The trans-Pacific trade of the entire United States is already half as much again as that across the Atlantic. Thus, if there is any proposal for an extension of regional free trade arrangements beyond the Western Hemisphere that would make sense for the America of the future, it is that which will eventually come out of the Asia-Pacific Economic Cooperation Forum, where the United States and the leaders of 14 other Pacific Rim nations have committed themselves to free trade and investment by the year 2020. It would make sense for both countries if Japan would become a full partner with the United States in translating this proposal into reality. When all this is taken together it is hard to argue with the judgment of Alan Greenspan, the chairman of the Federal Reserve, when he said that the fundamental economic situation of the United States today is better than it has been for decades.

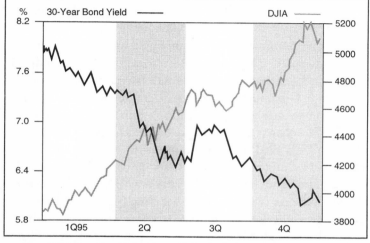

Figure 8.3 Source: *Barron's*, January 1, 1996. Reprinted by permission of *Barron's*, © 1996 Dow Jones & Company, Inc. All Rights Reserved Worldwide.

How will this very positive long-term outlook affect the financial markets in the United States in coming years? Let's start with interest rates, which are key. This is quite apparent from the chart above, which goes very far in explaining what happened to the stock market in 1995, when it had one of the strongest rises in its history. As long-term interest rates fell relentlessly, the stock market rose equally relentlessly. So the bull market of 1995 was quite obviously interest rate driven. But was a "bubble" developing along Japanese lines? It certainly looks that way to some observers. For them the early warning alarm bells started to ring in 1995, with the initial public offering (IPO) of the shares of Netscape Communications. Based in California, Netscape makes a software program called the Netscape Navigator that enables computer users to "browse" the World Wide Web, the graphical portion of the Internet. Because of the speed of the Navigator, the high quality of the graphics it relays to the home computer, and its ease of use, Netscape already controls 70 percent of a market consisting of an estimated ten million users and likely to expand.

In the original filing, Morgan Stanley, the lead underwriter, was going to issue 3.5 millon shares at $14 per share. Sensing the enormous interest, it increased the offer to 5 million shares and raised the price to $28 a share. With a total of 38 million shares outstanding, this would have put the market value of Netscape Communications at a shade over $1 billion. When trading in its shares was opened, however, the price immediately shot to $71 a share, boosting the company's market value to well over $2 billion. And this is a company that was just 15 months old, with revenues during the first six months of 1995 of only $85 million—and no profits. What was perhaps even more startling was that even after these sobering facts about Netscape became generally known among investors, the stock went to $150 a share. Had this been an isolated phenomenon it could have been shrugged off, but this was just a greatly exaggerated example of what was happening to the entire technology sector of the stock market in the United States. Other examples include Spyglass, another Internet company, which had no earnings and thus an incalculable P/E ratio, and whose stock price rose from $13 to $58 during the course of 1995; U.S. Robotics, a maker of modems with a P/E ratio of 55, whose stock price rose from $17 1/2 to $90; and Chiron, one of the world's leading biotech companies, which saw its stock price go from $47 to $111, while operating at a loss.

The *Financial Times,* in an editorial written under the title "Technology versus Tulips," compared what it termed the "technological mania" to the famous 17th-century tulip mania, the granddaddy of all speculative "bubbles," and drew the following conclusion:

> Technological stocks do at least have some advantage over tulips. A handful live up to the expectations that people invest in them. But if this is a bubble—*and it certainly looks,*

feels and floats like a bubble—such companies become cheaper when the bubble bursts. *It could happen when . . . bond yields rise.*[6]

This analysis may or may not be right. But assuming it is, would the bursting of the technology bubble bring the entire stock market down with it? That seems unlikely, because despite the overall steep rise in stock prices, corporate earnings have been more or less keeping pace. As a result, a key measure of the stock market, the average price/earnings (P/E) ratios of the stocks that make up either the Dow Jones Industrial Average or the S&P 500, did not appear to be out of line by historical standards. The 1960-94 average was 14 times earnings. By the end of 1995, the average P/E ratio of the Dow stocks was 15, or right in line with the historic norm.

So it has been the *combination* of falling interest rates and rising profits that has pushed up stock prices. But will interest rates continue to fall? Where short-term rates are concerned, the Federal Reserve has moved them down. The process began in July 1995 when, after raising the Federal Funds rate seven times in succession, the Federal Reserve reversed itself and reduced that rate from 6 percent to 5¾ percent. Subsequently it dropped the rate twice more to 5¼ percent. The likelihood is that it will stay near this rate for a while.

The outlook for long-term rates is more cloudy. In early 1996 we saw long-term rates bottom out after dropping to the lowest levels in two decades. After that, they began a steady rise. This rise could continue, if, as expected, modest economic growth continues. This would mean that one of the main forces that drove the stock market in the United States to ever higher levels—falling *long*-term interest rates—would disappear. A more modest rate of economic growth in the future, as compared to the past few years, would tend to diminish corporate profits, the other force that has been driving the market. The conclusion is that the U.S. stock market is in the process of temporarily topping out.

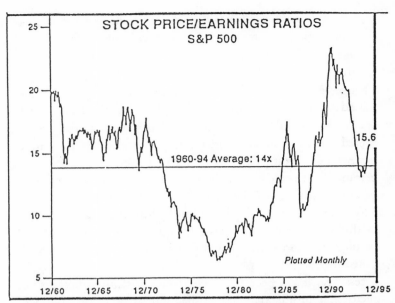

Figure 8.4 Source: *Wright Investor's Newsletter,* December 1995. Reprinted by permission of Wright Investor's Service.

If the possibility of the technological bubble bursting as a result of rising bond yields is included, as the *Financial Times* suggested, we would then be faced with the real possibility that the overall stock market in the United States would not just top out but start to move radically in the other direction. Could this result in a repeat of what happened in October 1987 when the DJIA plunged over 500 points in one day? This could not be ruled out completely if a financial crisis on Wall Street—triggered by a bursting of the technological bubble—led to an international dollar crisis, with the dollar going into a free-fall along the lines suggested in the "worst case" scenario. A number of other stock markets were hit by a crisis of confidence in 1995 in the wake of the collapse of the Mexican peso, the so-called "tequila effect," with the following results: Mexico, down 67.5 percent; Brazil, down 55.0 percent; Argentina, down 46.6 percent; Peru, down 37.4 percent; and Chile, down 22.4

percent. Would such a crisis of investor confidence also seriously change the *economic* outlook for the United States? Or, put another way, are the fundamentals of American economics strong enough to withstand such a financial crisis? My answer would be that they are.

That such financial events would lead to a temporary loss of consumer confidence in the United States is certain. That this would lead to a recession also seems likely, especially given the much lower rates of economic growth that would prevail prior to such a crisis of confidence. That this would interrupt the very optimistic perspective of the American economy described in this chapter is also certain. And finally, such a financial crisis would undermine efforts to balance the federal budget on schedule—as tax receipts fell and welfare costs rose in the pull of recession—meaning that the environment in which the private sector would have to work would be less benign than has been forecast here. But it would *not* require a total reassessment of the economic future of the United States by any means. All that has been said about the successful restructuring of American industry in the 1990s would remain valid. The high productivity enjoyed by the United States today—the highest in the world—would not be affected. Paradoxically, a renewed downward movement in the dollar's value would help exports, hinder imports, and thus reduce our trade deficit. Even the American banking system, which is sounder today than it has been in a long time, would remain strong, because, in contrast to Japan, the financial crisis caused by falling real estates prices—the S&L debacle—lies in America's past, not its future.

Most important, the long-term Schumpeterian forces that today drive the American economy—those provided by entrepreneurship, technological innovation, and venture capital—would remain alive and well and, in the end, prove much more lasting than the short-term forces of disruption that would follow an American financial crisis.

9

NOW LET'S TURN TO JAPAN.

The current views on the economic and financial outlook for Japan are divided into two radically different camps. This is best exemplified by the titles of two recent books about Japan published in the United States: Christoper Wood's *The End of Japan Inc.* and Eamonn Fingleton's *Blindside: Why Japan Is Still on Track to Overtake the U.S. by the Year 2000*. In short, there seems to be no middle ground. One group believes that Japan is finished; another believes that it is just marking time before moving onward and upward in the future, just as it did at the end of the 1960s and again at the end of the 1970s, after being knocked back by the oil shock.

The view that Japan is finished has been summed up as well as anywhere in the following two opinions, one voiced by a famous Wall Street investment banker, the other by the editorial writers of the *Wall Street Journal*. The investment banker, Barton Biggs, chairman of Morgan Stanley Asset Management, said:

> Japan is now just another mature industrial economy with a
> very overvalued currency, not the super-country some people
> raved about a couple of years ago. Besides, with earthquakes,
> a rotten banking system, political gridlock, and a full quota
> of crazies, Japan seems far less stable than it used to.[1]

The *Wall Street Journal* editorial ran under the title "Japan, Eek:"

> Today's Japan is not the economic powerhouse that gripped
> the conventional wisdom five years ago. Instead, it is the

most fragile major member of an interdependent world economy.

. . . It is mired in recession with little prospect of recovery. Internal demand is stifled by the usual oppressive taxes and regulations, and the overvalued yen makes an export-led recovery unlikely. Enormous losses have been suffered on domestic stocks and real estate, and also on heady foreign investments such as Rockefeller Center and Columbia Pictures. Naturally, especially given the cross-ownership that was supposed to be the wave of the future, this reflects itself in an imperiled banking system.

In the face of all this, the Bank of Japan declares itself helpless. It has cut interest rates and boosted the money supply, but can't stem deflation (or as the Japanese call it, "price destruction").

. . . Maybe the Bank of Japan really is helpless to do more; perhaps it can't push on a string. With fiscal policy also at something of an impasse and politics in turmoil, this leaves a bleak picture indeed. With no upside and a shaky banking system, in Japan we seem to be witnessing an economic phenomenon new to the postwar world. The string-pushing metaphor, indeed, comes straight out of the monetary policy debates of the Depression era.

The editorial then goes on to criticize President Clinton and his trade policy vis-à-vis Japan, ending with this warning to him: "If you implement trade sanctions, you are volunteering to take the political blame for any economic implosion in Japan and the shock waves this would send through the world economy."[2]

The editorial uses strong words: "depression," "the most fragile member of [the] world economy," "economic implosion."

The immediate causes of the fragility of the Japanese economy from 1992 to early 1996 were its overvalued currency and its seriously troubled banking system. In fact, these two were themselves interrelated. Were the yen to move back up again, it would probably lead to renewed deterioration in both stock and land prices and thus make an early resolution of the banking crisis more difficult.

Americans found out how a banking crisis could affect them when the country's savings and loan (S&L) industry collapsed in the late 1980s. The collapse was a major factor contributing to the United States' deepest recession since World War II, resulting in rates of unemployment that approached double digits in states such as California. The cause of the collapse was related to real estate and the fact that the entire thrift industry had misjudged the direction of interest rates, making 30-year loans at 7 percent and financing them by borrowing short-term at 4 percent. But when short-term rates skyrocketed (some S&Ls ended up paying as much as 14 percent for money), the total borrowing costs of the S&Ls were soon way above their interest income, meaning that it was only a matter of time before they collapsed. They had made the classic mistake of borrowing short and lending long. The final nail in their collective coffin came when American real estate prices started to move down, meaning that their collateral disappeared. The cost of the S&L bailout eventually totalled hundreds of billions of dollars, all borne by the American taxpayers. But there were remarkably few complaints. Most Americans knew that lack of government intervention would have only resulted in even more serious economic consequences for the entire nation.

The current Japanese banking crisis has been building up for years, its origins dating back to the collapse of land and stock prices as both of those bubbles burst at the beginning of the decade. For a while, it seemed that the Japanese were simply ignoring the potential consequences of this collapse for the banking system, hoping that a revival of those prices driven by a revival in the overall economy lay just around the corner. In *The End of Japan Inc.*, Christopher Wood describes the self-denial that was still alive as late as mid-1993: "On June 10, 1993, Hajime Fuada, then head of the official Economic Planning Agency (EPA), told the Japanese cabinet he was sure the economy has hit bottom'—just as his predecessor had done the previous year."[3] Wood points out that this opinion reflected the views of most of the key government policymakers in Japan, who had continued for far too long to regard the recession that began in 1992 as a normal cyclical adjustment. Their response, therefore, was strictly conventional: two major fiscal expansions that took place in September 1992 and March 1993 worth collectively ¥23.9 trillion ($240 billion) and primarily devoted to boosting public works expenditures. But as Wood points out:

> Such fiscal stimulus, however, has only succeeded in preventing the economy from entering into an outright freefall. Growth will at best remain marginal until the middle of this decade. That this is not a normal Japanese-style recession is already clear. . . . Far from recovering, the recession is actually getting worse.[4]

Subsequent events have proven Wood right. And the consequences for the banks have been devastating. As land prices continued falling, with the stock market still depressed and with no signs of economic recovery, many institutions gradually slipped toward insolvency. Like the Japanese officials, the bankers were very slow to admit it. Throughout 1993 and 1994, after writing off billions of dollars in debt, their estimates of the remaining bad debts of Japan's top 21 banks remained at or below ¥15 trillion ($150 billion). In June 1995, however, the Japanese government for the first time came out with an official estimate of the banks' problem loans that came closer to the truth: ¥40 trillion ($470 billion)—6 percent of all Japanese bank loans. At the peak of the S&L crisis in the United States in June 1991, bad loans accounted for only 5.6 percent of all bank lending in the United States. So even these official estimates signal that Japan's banking crisis represents a potentially bigger burden on its economy than the S&L debacle was on the economy of the United States. Moreover, many observers feel that the government is still deliberately underestimating the size of the problem. For example, Yukiko Ohara of UBS Securities has said that the bad

Vulnerable Banks

Salomon Brothers estimate of problem loans at some large Japanese institutions

BANK	MINIMUM PROBLEM LOANS (trillions yen)	PERCENTAGE OF OUTSTANDING LOANS
Nippon Trust & Banking	0.29	16.6
Nippon Credit Trust Bank	1.13	10.6
Yasuda Trust & Banking	0.84	8.6
Mitsui Trust & Banking	1.00	8.6
Sumimoto Trust & Banking	1.08	8.1
Hokkaido Takushoku Bank	0.56	7.7
Long-Term Credit Bank of Japan	1.32	7.0
AVERAGE 21 TOP BANKS	—	5.6

Figure 9.1 Source: *The Wall Street Journal,* May 12, 1995, p. A10. Reprinted by permission of *The Wall Street Journal,* © 1995 Dow Jones & Company, Inc. All Rights Reserved Worldwide.

debt of all Japanese banks will grow to ¥100 trillion ($1.2 trillion)—nearly a quarter of Japan's annual economic output.

Salomon Brothers has listed some of the most vulnerable banks and the degree of their vulnerability. These, and all the other banks that have found themselves in similar dire straits, have had no choice but to retrench. The problem first surfaced in June 1994, when, for the first time in postwar Japanese history, Japan's banks reported that their outstanding loans had shrunk from levels of a year earlier. Lending continued to fall throughout 1995, and as lending fell, the banks' interest income declined and with it the profit they needed to finance write-offs of bad loans. These bad loans have weakened Japan's banks to the point where many have lost their ability to lend to struggling companies that need money. The chain of events can be seen in the graphs in figure 9.2.

Then, in the summer of 1995, the situation got even worse. On July 31 a run started on the Cosmo, the big Tokyo credit union, triggered by a newspaper report that the financial institution had a huge amount of nonperforming loans on its books. Within three days, ¥91 billion ($1 billion), or one-fifth of the financial institution's deposits, were withdrawn. As the

Falling Land Prices
% chg central-Tokyo

Weak Stock Prices
Daily Nikkei 225 Close

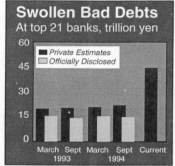

Swollen Bad Debts
At top 21 banks, trillion yen

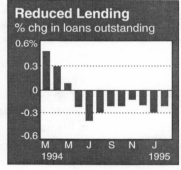

Reduced Lending
% chg in loans outstanding

Figure 9.2 Source: Jathon Sapsford and Michael Williams, "Japan's Bank Mess: Three Years, Still Digging," *The Wall Street Journal,* May 25, 1995, p. A10. Reprinted by permission of *The Wall Street Journal,* © 1995 Dow Jones & Company, Inc. All Rights Reserved Worldwide.

Economist described the situation, "The collapse of this would-be bank was scary. Even a system that is fundamentally healthy can be brought low by runs, once that psychology takes hold. And right now Japan's financial system is anything but healthy." The result was that both the Japanese *and* the American monetary authorities were shocked into taking decisive action to stabilize the financial situation. The Japanese central bank, the Bank of Japan (BoJ), made an emergency loan to Cosmo to allow it to meet withdrawals, an action it had not taken since 1965 when it bailed out Yamaichi, a stockbrokerage company. Breaking with previous policy, the Americans now joined the Japanese in repeated intervention in the foreign exchange market to weaken the yen and prop up the dollar. Both actions were successful. The run on Cosmo was stopped on August 3, and by the end of the month, the yen had been pushed down to 100 to the dollar, the lowest it had been in almost half a year. This crisis was over.

Just weeks later, however, a new crisis arose. This time it did not involve a relatively small, obscure financial institution in Tokyo, but rather the huge Daiwa bank with its worldwide operations, including 20 branches in the United States. On September 15, the management of the New York branch of Daiwa informed U.S. regulators that they had just discovered a $1.1 billion loss that the bank had suffered due to the unauthorized activities of one of its bond traders, Toshihide Iguchi. It subsequently was revealed that these losses had been accumulating over an 11-year period. To conceal this, Daiwa's New York management had begun a policy as early as 1989 of temporarily relocating bond traders and their record keeping to another building in advance of the arrival of auditors at the main branch in New York. On July 17, 1995, Iguchi sent a confession letter to Daiwa's headquarters in Japan, admitting to the $1.1 billion loss. He followed this with a second letter outlining ways to cover up the scandal by, for instance, transferring all the accounts involved to Daiwa's branch in the Cayman Islands. All agreed to keep the trading loss secret until November, but in a change of heart, Daiwa informed Japanese regulators about the entire mess on August 8. Finally, on September 15, they told U.S. regulators, and a week later Iguchi was arrested in New York and charged with fraud.

The Federal Reserve was understandably furious that both Daiwa and the Japanese government had kept all this concealed and later ordered that Daiwa close all 20 of its American branches. The entire global financial community was understandably shocked at the gross mismanagement of Daiwa that had led to this immense loss, which raised questions about whether similar situations existed, undetected or at least unadmitted, in other major Japanese banks. As a result, Japanese banks now had to pay a premium when bidding for deposits, both dollars and yen, in London or New York. This meant that their costs of funds was now one-third of one percent higher than that of its foreign competitors in other countries.

The seriousness of the situation caused the BoJ to take an unprecedented action in late October 1995, requesting that the Federal Reserve act as the lender of last resort to all 20 Japanese commercial banks that had operations in the United States; the Fed agreed to do so. As a result, at any hour of the day or night the Fed will let the BoJ swap U.S. government paper for dollars to use in resolving any sudden cash crises involving Japanese banks. This was meant to buy time by reassuring financial markets that the Fed stood behind the BoJ at a time when Japanese politicians were still reluctant to take the steps necessary to put their banks on a sound footing. To be sure, the Fed was also acting to protect American interests. By dealing off-market via swaps, Japanese sellers of U.S. Treasury paper would not have to disrupt money markets in New York and suddenly drive up U.S. interest rates. A side deal was also entered into under which both central banks agreed to stabilize the yen/dollar exchange rate in the range of 100 to 105.

In December 1995, the Japanese government finally began to do what it should have done years earlier. It introduced a plan for a government bailout of failing banks modelled along the lines of the Resolution Trust Corporation (RTC), which, in the early 1990s, managed to resolve America's savings and loan crisis within a remarkably short time by taking over and then reselling a half trillion dollars of assets of defunct S&Ls. In addition, the BoJ slashed interest rates, allowing banks in Japan to make a killing on their holdings of government bonds (which rise in price as interest rates fall), just as the American Federal Reserve did in the early 1990s. As in America, the windfall profits accruing to Japanese commercial banks can now be used to replenish their capital bases, which have been so badly undermined by the necessity of making massive write-offs of bad real estate loans.

This process proved hugely successful in the United States, where the banking system was restored to health within five years and, as a result, is today in excellent shape.

Although the Japanese are relieved that the government is finally taking action, they realize that putting the banking system back into shape will take much longer in Japan than it did in the United States. The American RTC was able to move in on sick S&Ls with great speed simply by declaring them bankrupt, appointing themselves the receivers of the assets, and then bundling together such assets and selling them. By contrast, Japan's RTC will have to ask for a bankruptcy order from a court, which will then appoint lawyers as receivers. Japan's legal system is notoriously slow, and its attorneys have no experience in dealing with failed banks. Furthermore, while in America the RTC could move ahead quickly because it was able to repackage bad loans and sell them as securities, in Japan such "securitization" was not allowed until mid-1996. Finally, the rebuilding of the banks' capital bases will be hampered by yet another reform, namely a *sevenfold* increase in the premiums Japanese banks must pay to the nation's deposit insurance system. Such premium costs will be significantly higher than in any other industrialized nation. This is, however, considered by many to be the central component of this overall government package designed to stabilize Japan's troubled financial system, since the cost of repaying depositors of the five banks that have already collapsed far exceeds the sums available at the Deposit Insurance Corporation.

All this is absolutely necessary if the Japanese banking system is to eventually return to health. Doubts about its overall efficacy still remain. Thus, in the closing days of 1995, even after all these measures had been announced, the Standard and Poor Rating Group lowered the ratings of four of Japan's strongest banks. In doing so, S&P said that strong banks will still have to bear much of the costs related to the failures of small and medium-sized institutions, since public money will be used to bail out only credit unions and specialized mortgage lenders and not banks. It further warned that the beefed-up deposit insurance system probably won't be enough to cover future failures of financial institutions. So the problems of Japan's financial system will continue to cast a pall over the entire Japanese economy in the foreseeable future.

In the meantime, the problems could start to get worse if the yen, after its recent respite, begins to rise again. Remember how totally out of kilter the yen/dollar exchange rate had become relative to "fundamentals" in 1995. If you take the 1995 GDP of Japan and translate it into dollars at $1=¥79, where the yen stood at its apex in the spring of that year, you get a dollar equivalent of $5.4 trillion, or about the same size as the United States economy. Nobody believes that that comes even close to reality.

This brings us to *purchase power parity* (PPP). The theory behind PPP is that goods should cost the same in all countries when measured in a common currency. The PPP is thus the exchange rate that equates the price of a basket of identical trade goods and services in two countries. Goldman Sachs, the U.S. investment bank, has calculated that the dollar's current PPP is ¥185. The OECD puts it at ¥ 181. By translating Japan's GDP into dollars at those rates, you get a Japanese economy that is somewhere between one-half and three-fifths the size of the American economy. Common sense tells you that this appears about right.

If you use PPP to measure per capita GDP, you get similar results. Three countries—Luxembourg, the United States, and Switzerland—are clustered in the lead, followed, with a substantial lag, by Japan. Again, common sense tells you that this probably comes very close to reflecting reality. If exchange rates were to be realigned to conform to that reality, it would mean a massive—at least 50 percent—devaluation of the yen and an equally massive revaluation of the dollar.

Is there a possibility that reality, as reflected in these PPPs, will win out in the end? The *New York Times* recently featured an economist with Capital Investments International, Bob Barbera, who argues that it will. Barbera says that a "death dance" was being performed by the yen and the Nikkei, the Japanese stock market, in 1995. His chain of reasoning:

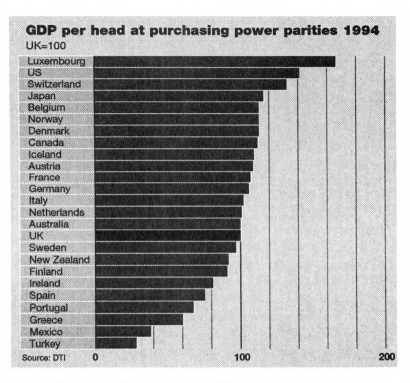

GDP per head at purchasing power parities 1994
UK=100

Luxembourg
US
Switzerland
Japan
Belgium
Norway
Denmark
Canada
Iceland
Austria
France
Germany
Italy
Netherlands
Australia
UK
Sweden
New Zealand
Finland
Ireland
Spain
Portugal
Greece
Mexico
Turkey

Source: DTI   0   100   200

Figure 9.3 Source: *The Financial Times,* May 25, 1995. Reprinted by permission of *The Financial Times* © 1995. All Rights Reserved Worldwide.

- Japan's trade surplus generates enormous foreign exchange reserves.
- Japan's banks cannot recycle this cash, given their impaired financial state.
- Yen appreciation results.
- A rising yen puts pressure on the Nikkei.
- Falling equity prices put further pressure on Japanese banks.
- Japan's banks pull capital home, to make up for capital shortfalls caused by the falling Nikkei.
- Yen appreciation results.

Japan: Nikkei Share Price Index vs. Yen per US$

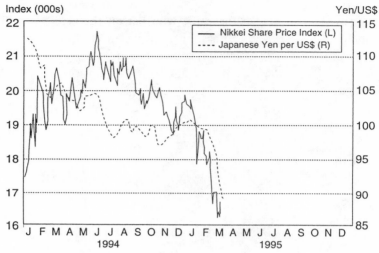

Figure 9.4   Source: Capital Investment Fund.

Barbera then asked: "What can stop this terrible tango?" His answer:

> A change in the underlying real economy fundamentals. Yen appreciation, one must recall, also changes the relative prices of Japanese goods and the relative costs of Japanese labor. Given today's yen level, list prices on goods in Japan are now 110% higher than in New York, London, or Rome. In addition, unit labor costs in Japan are well over 50% higher than in the U.S. Look for the recent swelling of import volumes flowing into Japan to accelerate. Watch for rising Japanese export prices. Expect the volume of the trade to swing sharply over the next two years. The fact that this has not yet happened is testimony to the resilience of Japanese corporations and endurance of Japanese workers. But the Nikkei/yen death dance seems destined to annihilate the trade surplus.[5]

Mr. Barbera concludes, in the *New York Times*, that the yen is a "boomerang currency," arguing that when it starts to fall, it will do so rapidly, devastating those who bet on the yen. But he won't forecast a date. He says, "The most powerful thing about speculative markets at the end is that they are going up because they are going up. Once they start going down, you remember a whole host of reasons why they should never have gone up that much to begin with."

Barbera is not alone in making such an argument. Richard Koo, an economist with Nomura Research Institute in Tokyo, says: "The strong yen is made in Japan almost 100%. The US is basically powerless to affect the $/yen rate." In London's *Financial Times*, this argument was expanded as follows:

> The most important cause of the appreciation of the yen is the country's success as an exporter. This creates an enormous current account surplus with the rest of the world— $129.3bn in 1994 (and an average of around $90bn for each of the four previous years.) The companies that earn these dollars ultimately require yen cash to pay domestic workers, suppliers and shareholders, so they are a structural source of dollar selling. Unlike speculators or investors, they cannot change and become dollar buyers.[6]

But why was the dollar/yen crisis so late in coming? Because in the past, that surplus had been counterbalanced by net exports of long-term capital by the private sector. But conditions have changed since, making overseas investments less attractive to Japanese investors for a variety of reasons. First, there were huge foreign exchange losses on foreign investment, described earlier in this book. Second, there was the collapse of assets prices in Japan when the bubbles burst, removing the buffer provided by unrealized capital gains on stocks and real estate that investment managers and banks enjoyed in the 1980s. More recently came the fall in foreign interest rates, exemplified by the 30-year U.S. Treasury bonds. At one point in the 1980s the yield for these bonds was 14 percent. By 1995 it was less than half that. As Philip Gawith has noted,

> The cumulative effect of these trends has been a massive withdrawal by Japanese investors from foreign markets. But if the supply of dollars through the current account surplus remains steady, while the demand for dollars from Japanese offshore investors drops, the yen can only rise.

What can stop that rise?

> First, the sharp rise in the yen should, in the long run, narrow the trade gap, by increasing the price of exports. Aside from domestic investors going abroad, the only [other] means of achieving balance between the demand for and supply of yen is by opening up domestic markets to imports, so that foreigners can earn yen.[7]

What both observers seem to agree on, then, is that the future of the yen will depend upon some combination of these three factors: a major downward shift in Japanese exports, a major upward shift in Japanese imports, and a revival in Japanese foreign investment.

There has been a minor revival in 1995-96, stemming from the huge gap that opened up between interest rates available in Japan in the yen and those available in other countries in other currencies. Most illustrative of what was happening was a practice that developed among professional Japanese traders, who borrowed yen very short-term in London at interest rates less than 1 percent, exchanged them for dollars, and then bought 30-year U.S. Treasury bonds, which were yielding 6.5 percent. As the yield fell to 6 percent and the prices of the bonds rose accordingly, the traders generated profits that they could never have made had they stayed at home.

The *Wall Street Journal,* in a lead article, developed the same theme under the headline "Tired of Poor Returns, Many

Japanese Send Their Savings Abroad." But the fine print of the article revealed, "So far, however, Japan is shipping only a thin slice of its savings overseas. About 88% of its $9.4 trillion in household financial assets is in domestic institutions. And its small investors could quickly stop sending money abroad if foreign bonds prove risky; another surge in the yen could wipe out the value of foreign holdings not denominated in yen." Where Japanese purchases of foreign securities are concerned, the statistics can be misleading on the surface since there were huge net Japanese purchases of foreign securities in 1994 and 1995, running into the tens of billions of dollars. Most of that, however, came from purchases by Japanese investors of Euro-yen bonds, which count as overseas assets in the payments figures. Thus since 1994 PepsiCo has sold Euro-yen bonds worth 42 billion yen, or about $420 million, to Japanese investors. The government of Mexico raised 100 billion yen by issuing Euro-yen bonds, and Italy has likewise issued huge amounts of yen-denominated securities. For the issuer, this practice arises from the fact that they have to pay on average three to four percentage points less on Euro-yen borrowing than they would have had to pay had they issued dollar bonds. For the Japanese investor, this type of "foreign" investment is attractive because despite the fact that Euro-yen interest rates are low by international standards, they are higher than they could get at home, and they carry no currency risk. Huge, multibillion issuances of Euro-yen bonds have continued in 1996. As Japanese investors are offered more and more high-quality, off-shore yen bonds as a means of recycling the country's continuing current account surplus, they will continue to shun dollar-denominated securities.

Where real estate is concerned, the exodus from the United States continues. Between 1985 and 1991 Japanese companies invested about $77 billion in U.S. property. We have already discussed two such investments—Rockefeller Center and the Pebble Beach resort, both of which resulted in enormous losses when the Japanese investors finally sold out and took their money back home. But these were just the two most spectacular examples on a list that gets longer and longer. For example:

- *Hotel Bel-Air:* A Tokyo hotel company bought the hotel for $119 million in 1989 and sold it in 1994 for $60 million.
- *The Galleria:* Mitsubishi Bank lent the American developer of this shopping center $94 million. It later sold the loan for $6 million after the developer defaulted.
- *Hyatt Regency Waikoloa:* Mitsubishi lent $400 million to the developer of this Hawaiian resort. In 1993 it sold the defaulted loan for $60 million.
- *Financial Square:* Sanwa Bank loaned $350 million to the developer of this New York office building. Sanwa recently foreclosed and sold the loan for $130 million.

On top of these losses came the currency losses. It is no wonder, then, that Japanese investors in American real estate have simply had enough.

The *Financial Times* has estimated that in 1993-94 combined, Japanese owners sold $4.5 billion worth of American property. This increased to $7 billion in 1995. This process was stepped up even further in 1996, with Japanese sellers still lined up in places such like Hawaii, hoping to finally be able to unload hotel and resort properties, even at tremendous losses. Such disinvestment is expected to continue at a rate of $5 to $10 billion a year over the next three to five years.

The exceptions to this minor revival in Japanese purchases of foreign securities, and the continued exodus from foreign real estate, are the major purchases of U.S. government securities by the BoJ. As it purchased massive amounts of U.S. dollars in the foreign exchange market in order to prop up its value against the yen, BoJ invested those dollars—approximately $100 billion in 1995—in U.S. government securities. According to some observers, the yield on the 30-year Treasury bonds would

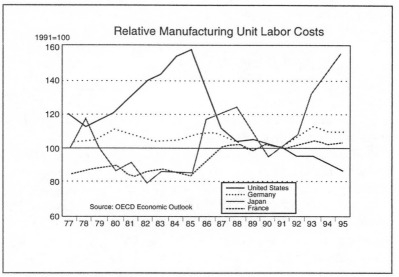

Figure 9.5 Source: Capital Investment Fund.

have been 0.25 to 0.50 percentage points higher without such Japanese purchases. With the BoJ now the largest foreign holder of dollars, with an amount estimated at $200 billion, there are questions as to how many more it will be willing to accumulate. Should BoJ restrict future purchases, the major force that pushed the yen from 79 back down to well over 100 to the dollar will no longer be present.

So what about exports and imports? It seemed inevitable that Japanese exports would fall and imports rise as a result of what happened to the yen. This brings us to the inverse J-curve.

The J-curve is the phenomenon that accounts for the fact that although the whole world knows that Japanese trade surpluses have been ballooning in recent years, they "know" so because the trade figures they look at are denominated in U.S. dollars. However, if they were to look at what has been happening to that same trade surplus when measured in yen, they would be surprised to find out that it has been plunging during the past three years. In yen terms, the Japanese trade surplus had already peaked in 1992 at ¥16,752 billion. Two years later it fell to ¥14,876 billion. In the first quarter of 1995, a further fall of 13 percent in the trade surplus was recorded, and as a result of a widening service deficit, the overall current account surplus was down by 20 percent.

All this can be explained by currency movements. While Japan's surpluses have indeed been falling when measured in yen, that currency has, of course, been soaring against the dollar. The rise has been so great that the surplus in dollars kept rising to a record peak in 1994 of $145 billion. This is because although a higher yen raises the prices of Japanese exports and eventually reduces foreign demand for them, thereby reducing the trade surplus, it takes many months for the increase in export prices to work its way through the system. In the meantime, export volume remains unchanged while its value increases. Exactly the opposite is true for Japanese imports, since the immediate effect of a rising yen was to lower total import values.

By 1996, the effects of the high yen in 1994-95 should have worked their way through the system, and Japanese exports, even in dollar terms, should be suffering accordingly. But the consequences have not been as severe as might have been expected on the basis of the experience of the United States in the 1980s when the overvalued dollar devastated U.S. industry.

For although Japan's export growth in dollar terms slowed to 7 percent in the year ending March 1996, it did not stop. What happened was that the direction of Japan's exports shifted from the United States and Europe to Asia. So although Japan's trade surplus with the U.S. shrank by 27 percent, with Asia it rose by 17 percent. The biggest change can be found in Japanese imports. They increased by over 18 percent in dollar terms.

Taken together, this means that the Japanese overall trade surplus is finally also falling in dollar terms as Japan rounds the bend of the inverse J-curve. The overall trade surplus of Japan shrank by 18.4 percent to $96 billion in the year ending March

Japan: Balance of Payments

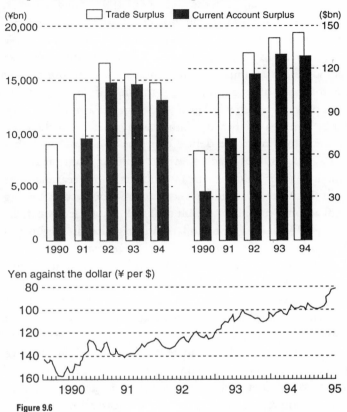

(¥bn)   ☐ Trade Surplus   ■ Current Account Surplus   ($bn)

Yen against the dollar (¥ per $)

Figure 9.6

1996. It will probably continue to shrink as imports rise still further, a result of a consumption-driven economic recovery fueled by extremely low interest rates and a fiscal policy designed to provide classic Keynesian stimulus.

And what will now happen to the yen? As many experts have discovered, it is sheer folly even to attempt to forecast where exchange rates are headed. If you had taken a poll of American bankers and economists at the end of 1994, the vast majority would have forecasted a rising dollar for 1995 and beyond. Similarly, most Japanese in the first half of 1995 would have said that the yen was headed still higher. Both forecasts proved wrong. Having said that, what would seem to be a possible scenario for the dollar/yen exchange rate during the next two years? Some central imponderables must be kept in mind. Will these forecasts of a continuing shrinking of Japanese trade surplus prove right? Or will Japan's exports once again surge as its industry remakes itself in the future as it has done in the past? Will the American trade deficit continue to shrink, as it has recently, as a result of export growth stemming from the highly competitive position of American products in overseas markets? Or will the American academic economists who predict a rising current account surplus as a result of shrinking budgetary deficits prove right? Will the glut of dollars in foreign hands continue to grow, leading to a "financial crisis" as the *Economist* suggests? Or will the Bank of Japan continue to recycle surplus dollars, thus staving off any such crisis indefinitely?

A possible scenario is this: First, there will be a continuing lull in the foreign exchange market. Next, the yen will gradually move up to the 90 to 100 range as neither the American deficits nor the Japanese surpluses shrink as much as had been hoped for. This could provoke another round of currency speculation pushing the yen still higher, which would be met by unprecedented central bank intervention, this time including intervention by the United States. By 1997, as the Japanese economy moves into a genuine recovery, and as Japan, therefore, begins to slide even further down the inverted J-curve, the yen will move into what may prove to be the longer-term equilibrium level of 90 to 100 to the dollar.

Turning to the longer term outlook for Japan's economy, there can be no doubt that if the trade surplus continues to diminish in size, leading to a stable yen in the 90 to 100 range, the lack of investor confidence in Japanese stocks, as reflected in the Nikkei remaining at almost 50 percent below its peak level at the beginning of the decade, will gradually be replaced by long-term optimism. Attention will return to the fundamental strengths of the Japanese economy, which support the thesis that the half-decade-long interruption of economic growth in Japan has come to an end.

Ultimately, Japan needed this crisis of confidence, just as America needed the crisis of confidence that occurred at the end of the 1980s and climaxed in the recession that followed. It led to a major restructuring of business and finance in the United States and was followed by five years of solid growth in both output and employment. It has also ultimately led to the realization by the political leadership in the United States that something has to be done to eliminate the nation's chronic budget deficits; something has to be done to increase the nation's rate of savings, lest the country sink back into an even more serious crisis of confidence.

The restructuring required in Japan, however, is of a different nature. As seen from the outside, what is required are concrete and consistent reforms aimed at a voluntary opening of the Japanese market to competition, especially competition from abroad. As a result, Japan will become a consumer-driven culture more like that of all the other industrialized countries of the West. This would require that Japan recognize that it represents the last major industrialized country on earth that still has at its core a system of central planning run by intransigent bureaucrats who will continue to insist that Japan is "different" until they are replaced by a new generation who knows better.

As William Dawkins has pointed out in the *Financial Times,* Kenichi Ohmae, one of Japan's best known management consultants and the founder of the political group Reform of Hesei, is a leading advocate of the argument that Japan is, or at least should be, on the threshold of such a sudden change. Ohmae believes that the jerky progress of modern Japanese history supports the thesis that Japan tends to move in jumps after periods of crisis. The 19th-century Meiji restoration, for example, in which Japan turned from medieval feudalism into an industrialized country in a few decades, followed a period of civil strife. Similarly, Japan's recent economic miracle came after World War II and the occupation by the United States. Today, argues Ohmai, the growth of communications has undermined the government's ability to protect the Japanese economy from international rivals. This will lead to more competition flowing into the still protected parts of the economy, which will lead to the required restructuring and long-term revival of the Japanese economy.

There is another school of thought, that of the so-called revisionists. Chief among them are Professor Chalmer Johnson, author of *Japan: Who governs?*; James Fallows, author of *Looking at the Sun: The Rise of the New East Asian Economic and Political System*; Eamonn Fingleton, author of *Blindside*; and Karel van Wolfern, author of *The Enigma of Japanese Power*. Their thesis is that Japan's political and economic structure favors status quo over change, powerful producers over weak consumers, huge trade surpluses over balanced trade. This will never change unless constant pressure is applied from the outside. They argue further that Japan's huge trade surpluses allow it to pile up wealth and grow strong at the expense of the United States. So from the Japanese point of view, the "system" is superior to that of the United States in particular and the West in general and thus does not warrant change. The revisionists say that for ten years, non-Japanese observers have debated whether Japan's economic juggernaut has finally hit the wall, whether the miracle is over because Japan's people are tired of belt tightening and because big Japanese corporations are too cumbersome for the agile new information age. But as James Fallows recently pointed out:

> above all they say that the steady rise of the yen's value will price Japanese exporters out of business as Toyotas and Sonys become too expensive for foreigners to buy.
>
> Ten years ago, one U.S. dollar was worth more than 250 yen. Over the next two years, the dollar's value against the yen plummeted—to 220 yen, then 180, then 120. And at every step of the way a chorus of Japanese and American

observers said: This is it! NOW Japanese exporters will face too great a price handicap. NOW America imports will be an irresistible bargain in Japan. NOW the trade imbalance will go away. But the dollar kept falling—below 90 last week—the yen kept rising, and the patterns of trade were virtually unchanged.

Throughout this process there has been a renegade, alternative view . . . [that] the higher the yen goes, the stronger—not weaker—Japan's industries will ultimately become. This view . . . has many components but its central idea is that the Japanese economy is organized in a way that channels the yen's new buying power largely into industrial investment. This in turn lets Japan's exporters keep pushing their costs down, through productivity increases, even faster than the yen goes up.[8]

Fallow's conclusion is that Japan will come out of this latest yen crisis stronger than ever; another economic comeback for Japan is inevitable.

A non-ideologist could well conclude that whether one accepts the more orthodox views of Kenichi Ohmae or those of the revisionists, the result is the same: Japan will come out of the 1995 dollar/yen crisis primed to move back onto a growth curve that will carry it well into the next century. Christopher Wood comes down on the side of the non-revisionists with arguments that are very persuasive. Wood says that rather than adamantly protecting the status quo, Japan's bureaucracy is moving, however slowly, however reluctantly, toward some sort of market solution of Japan's crisis. Applied to the corporate sector, this approach will mean sanctioning widespread layoffs, as the scrapping of excess production capacity in Japan takes place on a very large scale with employees released onto the labor market much more rapidly than the service sector can absorb them. Wood points out that with the yen at this high level, the ability of Japan's corporate sector to act as an unofficial welfare state, subsidizing more than 3 million underemployed workers, becomes harder to sustain every day. In fact, Japan's unemployment rate would probably already be 7 to 8 percent—instead of 3 to 4 percent—if the totem of lifelong employment had been abandoned. Wood feels that it soon will be, since the rigid employment system is the major obstacle for a Japanese economy that needs to respond more quickly to the competitive challenges posed by a world economy moving quickly into the information age. Wood argues:

> If Japan does not rise to this challenge, the country risks sharing the fate of America's IBM. And there are notable similarities between this former industrial powerhouse of an economy and the shrunken America corporate giant besides their long-shared adherence to paternalistic employment systems. Five years ago, IBM was too wedded to its own traditional belief systems to recognize the threat posed to its continued survival by fast-changing events in the outside world. After indulging in the absurd arrogance of the late 1980s Bubble, Japan's iron triangle of bureaucrats, businessmen and politicians has been equally slow in the 1990s to acknowledge the impending inevitability of deep structural change. For the old ways no longer work. *This time is really different.*[9]

Wood concludes that such change is now finally taking place and that, when this restructuring process is complete, "Japan will become a consumerist society with all the diversity of choice long taken for granted by spoiled Americans."

What will be the consequences of all this where financial markets are concerned? One is tempted to draw a parallel between where the Nikkei was in 1989 and where it is today and where the Dow Jones Industrial Average was before and after the October 1987 stock market crash. In August of 1987, the DJIA had peaked at 2,722. Sixty days later (after the crash on October 17, 1987, which took the market down over

500 points in one day), it bottomed out almost 1,000 points lower at 1,738. To be sure, this plunge was a precursor to the deepest American recession—which was to begin just a few years later—since World War II. But after the restructuring that occurred during that recession, America returned to an extended period of economic growth, and by the end of 1995, the Dow was well over 5,000.

Should Japan's approximately four years of economic stagnation end in 1996, with GDP growth returning to the 2.5 to 3 percent range, one could reasonably expect the Nikkei to begin to behave just like the Dow did in 1989 and beyond—to begin to trend decisively up. Aside from a turn-around in expectations that should finally begin to buoy investor confidence, two additional positive factors should influence the market. One is the enormously high liquidity that exists in Japan today. As the American investment bank Merrill Lynch has pointed out, three out of four times when liquidity reached current levels in Japan—in 1971, 1975, and 1986—the Nikkei rebounded. The second is the factor of portfolio diversification. Today Japan is grossly under-represented in the world's investment portfolios. Despite the partial recovery of the Nikkei, from its lows in the 14,000 range to back well above 20,000, the rise has been fueled predominantly by purchases by the managers of the huge portfolios of American mutual funds, British pension funds, and Swiss banks, rather than by domestic investors, leaving doubt as to its staying power. But as we near 1997, when an end to Japan's troubles may be finally in sight, the irrefutable fact will once again surface that Japan is, after all, the second largest economy in the world and is destined to remain that way for a long time. As its economy once again moves back onto a path of sustainable growth, the underrepresentation of its stocks in global portfolios will continue to be corrected, and domestic investors will return, adding another buoyant force to the market. Japanese bonds, on the other hand, may gradually lose their attraction as the deflationary process in

Japan comes to an end. The long-term investment strategy thus becomes: Go long on Japanese stocks. Get out of Japanese bonds. And avoid speculating on the yen/dollar relationship. The game is over.

10

LET'S NOW LOOK AT THE INTERNATIONAL MONETARY SYSTEM and the future roles of the dollar, the yen, and the deutsche mark as reserve currencies. Heretofore in our discussion of this issue we have concentrated almost exclusively on the dollar and the yen, just as we have similarly concentrated on the economic outlooks for Japan and the United States. But this ignores a third player in the game that constitutes a very powerful component: Western Europe in general, and Germany in particular. The relative size of a national economy, as measured in global terms, is a key determinant of how big a role its currency will play as a reserve currency. Today, Germany ranks third in the world in terms of GDP. The deutsche mark as a component of world currency reserves ranks second at around 16 percent. Within Europe, it is Germany and the deutsche mark that are at the heart of the nine-currency European Exchange Rate Mechanism (EMS) grid. Under the current rules, most currencies are allowed to fluctuate within 15 percent of agreed central rates against the other members of the mechanism. The exceptions are the deutsche mark and the guilder, which move in a 2.25 percent band. Recently, the gap between the weakest and the strongest currencies was just over 6 percent. This system has proven to be much less than ideal, and will hardly serve as a model for those who feel that the U.S. dollar and the yen should somehow be put into a super-grid with the deutsche mark in order to eliminate, or at least temper, future volatility in the exchange rates between these three key world currencies.

As history has already shown, if there is a sufficient disparity between economic and financial conditions of member

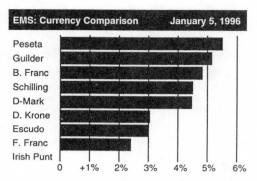

In the graph member currencies of the exchange rate mechanism are measured against the weakest currency in the system. Most of these currencies are permitted to fluctuate within 15 per cent of agreed central rates against the other members of the mechanism. The exceptions are the D-Mark and the guilder which are limited to movements within a 2.25 per cent band.

Figure 10.1

countries, speculators will move in and bust up the grid. The most spectacular example of this came in September 1992, when the grid was much narrower. Great Britain had put the pound sterling into the grid at a level (2.95) relative to the deutsche mark that was unsustainable. The speculators took on sterling, selling it short in massive amounts, and the Bank of England, which tried to defend it. The speculators won; sterling was forced out of the EMS, never to return again. A further example of the lack of dependability of the grid came in 1995, when, as a result of speculative raids, the Italian lira, the Spanish peseta, and the Portuguese escudo were all forced into major realignments relative to the deutsche mark. This contributed to the overall currency crisis of 1995, in that the intra-European flight to the safe-haven deutsche mark drove up its exchange value against the dollar at the same time as the yen was soaring against the dollar.

According to the OECD, such turbulence in the European currency markets damaged growth prospects for the EU in both 1995 and 1996, from original hopes of growth substantially above 3 percent to revised estimates of 3 percent or lower. The prospects for the German economy—the locomotive that drives all of Europe—were particularly shattered. The immediate twin threats to its economy came from a round of over-generous wage increases in 1995 coupled with a too strong deutsche mark. It was not just against the dollar that the Germany currency soared—from the DM 1.70 range to below DM 1.40 at times—but it also rose by an average of 7 percent against the currencies of all of its chief trading partners, most of which are in Europe.

All this currency turmoil came in addition to the fundamental difficulties in which Germany has found itself since the reunification of East and West Germany in 1992. It is now estimated that the cost of bringing former East Germany up to West German standards will require *two trillion deutsche marks,* or well over $1.4 trillion. This figure results from the fact that the entire infrastructure—roads, railroads, and telephone and electricity systems, all suffering from almost 50 years of total neglect—must be completely overhauled, and that on top of all this, eastern Germany is an environmental disaster. The required cleanup will dwarf the costs of the Chernobyl and Exxon Valdez disasters combined. There can be now no doubt that this will all take at least a decade to accomplish, and that the new provinces to the east will probably continue to be a burden on the rest of Germany for at least another decade. In this respect, Germany is something like Italy, whose southern part, the Mezzagiorno, has been massively subsidized by the north of Italy ever since the end of World War II, with no end in sight even today. The former West Germany will have to continue to make transfer payments of $120 billion a year for the rest of this decade, payments that must be financed both by higher taxes and by heavy government borrowing, a combination that hardly augurs well for sustained high rates of economic growth. In addition, if the economic situation in Eastern Europe deteriorates for whatever reason, and especially if Russia gets into serious trouble, it is going to be predominantly Germany that will have to provide the majority of the aid necessary to prevent chaos and the possible rise of a new form of irrational nationalism in the East. The former Yugoslavia provides an example of what is certainly possible elsewhere now that the lid on the pressure cooker imposed by the police state has been removed.

Germany must further overcome the rigidities that exist generally in the European economic system, rigidities that preclude that continent from going ahead with the restructuring that is necessary if it is to keep up with an already restructured America and a potentially restructured Japan. But in order to emulate an IBM, in order to be able to meet the new, fierce global competition, jobs must occasionally be sacrificed. And to fire *anybody* in France, or Belgium, or Italy is almost impossible.

It is not just rigidities in the labor market that cast a pall over Europe's future growth prospects. Government regulations do the same. An example is provided by Europe's giant pharmaceutical industry. It is imperative that industry keep technologically abreast with the rest of the world. Europe is already years behind both the United States and Japan in such key areas as telecommunications and computers and falling further behind every day. In the pharmaceutical industry, the future lies with biotechnology. But due to the strength of environmental groups in Germany or Switzerland, it will take years to get a permit to set up a biotech research facility—if one is ever granted—and another ten years to get a permit to set up a pilot plant. In the meantime the rest of the world will have left Europe's pharmaceutical industry in the dust. As already mentioned, Swiss pharmaceutical giants such as Hoffmann La Roche and Ciba-Geigy decided in the end that they had no choice but to go elsewhere, to places where they were welcome. This explains why both of these companies have invested many billions of dollars in biotech research and production facilities in Northern California. As a result, they will not only be employing American scientists, engineers, and technicians, but they will actually be financing a further widening of the gap between the United States and Europe in this key industry of the future.

Out of Work: Country by Country

Unemployment rates, 1993 to first quarter 1995.

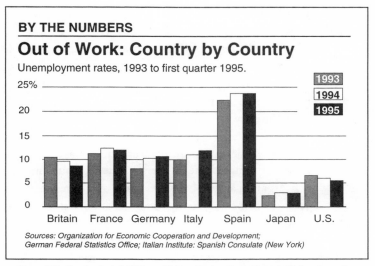

Sources: Organization for Economic Cooperation and Development;
German Federal Statistics Office; Italian Institute: Spanish Consulate (New York)

Figure 10.2   Source: Craig R. Whitney, "Jobless Legions Rattle Europe's Welfare States,"
The New York Times, June 14, 1995, p. A3. © 1995 The New York Times. Reprinted by
permission.

A further drag on the economic future of Europe is the
extremely heavy burden that all European enterprises must now
bear in regard to social benefits for their workers. In France, for
example, a company can hire a worker at minimum wage for
about $7 an hour ($1120 per month). But after it adds to that
what it must pay to the government in order to cover that
worker's social benefits, the monthly cost of that worker rises to
$1,800. And because in France, as in most other European
countries, the government will not allow employers to hire
part-time workers, employers hire no one at all. The net result of
this is massive unemployment throughout Europe on a scale not
seen since the Great Depression. The unemployment rates are
especially startling when compared with those of Japan and the
United States. In the long run, this situation will prove intolera-
ble. At some point it will lead to social unrest. So where does the
way out of this malaise lie? In 1957 it was the Treaty of Rome
that provided the framework for the European economic miracle | 1 4 1

of yesterday. It is now hoped that the Maastricht Treaty of 1991 will do the same for the Europe of tomorrow.

The key elements of this treaty were the provisions for the establishment of a common European currency under the aegis of a European central bank by no later than January 1, 1999. The economic arguments in favor of the establishment of a European Monetary Union (Emu) are based on the thesis that it is the final necessary step to boost to a higher level the efficiency of the single European market, which has already, for the most part, eliminated the barriers to the free movement of goods, services, and capital. Intra-EC trade and investment will become easier as exchange rate fluctuations disappear. In theory, the area covered by the Emu would turn into a vast domestic market free of competitive devaluation. The European currency unit would be to France and Germany what the United States dollar is to the states of New York and California—the common denominator of all monetary values.

The current schedule for the launch of the monetary union is as follows: The launch is to begin on January 1, 1999, but only if a sufficient number of member states are able to meet the convergence criteria (which we will describe later). Next, there will be an irrevocable locking of exchange rates, and a European central bank that will run the single monetary policy will be created. The new European currency, which will replace national currencies, will be named the "Euro," with a tentative timetable for the introduction of new notes and coins around the year 2002 or 2003.

According to the *Financial Times,* Yves-Thibault de Silguy, the European commissioner for monetary affairs who is the mastermind behind this plan, "has ruled out a 'Big Bang' approach to Emu whereby the replacement of national banknotes and coins would take place as soon as parities are fixed." Instead, he prefers a "mounting wave" approach that "would start with transactions between central and commercial banks and from there spill into national payment systems. He is pressing for large, computer-driven transactions in financial systems to take place fairly soon after the locking of exchange rates" with the aim of building up a "critical mass" of the single currency covering over 90 percent of the volume of monetary transactions. As the *Financial Times* concluded, his "unspoken goal is to persuade big financial institutions to invest in the new currency rather than the D-mark, still the currency king of Europe."[1]

The transition is not without hurdles. The creation of a common currency will lead to a myriad of legal difficulties covering the extension and enforceability of contracts previously valued in national currencies. There is also the question of how to set up a legally independent European central bank, a question to be answered by the EU heads of government between the end of 1997 and July 1998.

Many Europeans believe that their continent is now at a crossroads. The successful implementation of the monetary provisions of the Maastricht Treaty will give the EU exactly the boost it needs to begin to solve the most pressing problem facing all of Europe: unemployment. But failure to move to a common currency could endanger everything that the EU has done for Europe thus far. De Silguy put it bluntly, saying that without a single currency the single market would be in serious danger. His view echoes that of Ulrich Cartellieri, a director of Europe's most powerful bank, the Deutsche Bank, who says that failure to proceed with the European Monetary Union will have severe consequences for European currency stability, economic growth, and free trade. The *Financial Times* quoted him as saying that "The disappearance of the prospect of a joint currency would cause the EMS [European Monetary System] to break apart quickly and finally. Nor would the core of the EMS—the French franc/DM link—hold together any longer." The judgment then is that while the obstacles to success continue to appear very daunting, the concept of a European Monetary Union still enjoys the commitment of all of Europe's political leaders, with the exception of the British. The attitude of what seems to be a majority of the British was best voiced by former Prime Minister

Margaret Thatcher on the BBC: "I would say no single currency. This demeans Britain because we cease to have control either over the central bank or over our own currency." Thatcher believes that the United Kingdom should remain part of a European free trade area but opt out of any monetary union. Her views will certainly increase the already heavy pressure on Prime Minister John Major to commit the Conservative party before the next election against a single currency. This view was reenforced by the appointment of Malcolm Rifkind—who differs sharply with the Euro-enthusiasm of his predecessor, Douglas Hurd—as British Foreign Secretary. In his first major speech as foreign minister, Rifkind addressed the issue by saying that national interests must not be suppressed for the sake of "an artificial consensus on bogus unity," rejecting the concept of a "two-speed" Europe, since this implies "a common destination arrived at in different time scales" and ignores the fact that "there may be some areas of integration [a common currency] that even in the long term will not be attractive or acceptable to a number of member states."[2]

The key to the success of Emu, however, is not Great Britain but Germany, where there is also great public uneasiness about giving up the deutsche mark, a symbol of all that country has achieved since World War II. Chancellor Helmut Kohl, however, is convinced that the Emu is part of his life's work to anchor Germany once and for all in a united Europe. The new Gaullist government in France under Jacques Chirac seems as convinced as its socialist predecessors that the establishment of the Emu under the aegis of a new European central bank would break the current hegemony of the Bundesbank over European monetary policy. What they look forward to is a German-French co-hegemony, another reason why Britain may opt out.

The test will come soon, since the timetable for the achievement of a European Monetary Union is now more or less in place. Between the end of 1996 and July 1, 1998, a decision must be taken on which countries will qualify for the Emu. The

Maastricht Treaty sets very strict standards for countries that want to participate:

- The country's budget deficit may not exceed 3 percent of GDP.
- The country's debt to GDP ratio may not exceed 60 percent.
- The country's rate of inflation must not exceed 3.3 percent.
- The country's long-term interest rates must not exceed 9.3 percent.
- The country must have exhibited exchange rate stability as a participant in the Exchange Rate Mechanism.

The Institut für Weltwirtschaft in Kiel, Germany, has put together a forecast of how each of the 15 possible candidates will likely measure up to the Maastricht criteria in 1996. What becomes immediately apparent is that most of the European nations will miss some of the targets. Some nations, such as Italy and Spain, will miss *all* of them.

If the majority of the current members of the EU do not meet these criteria come July 1, 1997, or at the very latest January 1, 1999, then what—if anything—will happen? At present the "master plan" skirts this highly critical issue. Will the rules be bent in order to qualify the required majority of EU member countries? Or will an "inner core" of countries who do meet these standards be formed that will share a common currency under the aegis of a Frankfurt-based European Central Bank starting on January 1, 1999, with other member states being allowed to gradually trickle in if and when they meet the criteria? It is this latter procedure that appears most likely. The "inner core" will be made up of Germany, France, and the three Benelux countries—Belgium, the Netherlands, and Luxembourg. Belgium presents a problem, since it is still out of line in regard to both the deficit/GDP ratio and, more seriously, the debt/GDP ratio. But Belgian prime minister Jean-Luc Dehaene has pledged to put

1996 Maastricht Criteria
— Forecast —

	Inflation	Interest rate	Deficit /GDP	Debt /GDP	Exchange rate
Reference	3.3	9.3	-3.0	60	ERM-Participation
Germany	2.1	7.0	-2.2	58	Yes
France	1.7	7.3	**-4.1**	53	Yes
Italy	**4.7**	**11.4**	**-6.9**	123	No
United Kingdom	3.1	8.2	-2.6	54	No
Spain	**4.1**	**11.0**	**-5.5**	67	Yes
Netherlands	1.8	7.1	-2.1	**79**	Yes
Belgium	2.0	7.6	**-4.0**	**133**	Yes
Sweden	2.8	**10.9**	**-6.4**	**86**	No
Austria	2.5	7.1	**-3.9**	**67**	Yes
Denmark	3.0	8.7	-1.6	**75**	Yes
Finland	2.6	8.9	**-3.3**	**71**	No
Portugal	**4.2**	**9.9**	**-5.0**	**70**	Yes
Greece	**7.0**	**12.0**	**-10.0**	**114**	No
Ireland	3.0	8.2	-2.4	**82**	Yes
Luxembourg	2.0	—	1.2	7	Yes

In bold type: target missed

Table 10.1

a reduction in budget deficits at the top of his list of priorities for the express purpose of making it possible for Belgium to be one of the first countries to be a party to a single European currency. There are three additional countries that are on course to meet this key criterion: Denmark, Ireland, and Finland.

The odds today seem much higher than ever before that this eight-nation European currency bloc will become a reality on January 1, 1999. It will represent a formidable new player in the global economic, financial, and monetary arenas. In terms of total clout—population, GDP, and trade volume—it would rank somewhere between Japan and the United States. Based on that alone, it seems most probable that its currency would definitely gain stature as a reserve currency. This outlook is all the more likely if one considers that the guiding force behind this new currency will be Germany. In essence, the Euro will be a super deutsche mark. It will be managed just as the deutsche mark has been, meaning that the primary goal of the European central bank will be to keep inflation as close to zero as possible. As Jacques Santor has put it, it will be "a zone of monetary stability in a world of free capital movement." Its attractiveness as a reserve currency will be especially strong in Eastern Europe, just as the deutsche mark is today. Germany's trade with the former Eastern bloc already amounts to one-seventh of its total trade of 700 billion deutsche marks. As Eastern Europe completes its transition to the free enterprise system, that trade is bound to boom, and it will be denominated in the Euro, not the dollar. The result may be a "Euro currency zone" that will extend from the Atlantic almost to the Urals and beyond. If the deutsche mark's share in total central bank reserve is today in the 16 percent range, it is not unreasonable to expect that the Euro will end up with at least 20 percent early in the next century.

The role of the yen will grow for similar reasons. Japan is to Asia what Germany is to Europe, the difference being that Asia is the fastest growing region on earth. In a recent article in the *Economist,* the top five countries with the best growth prospects in this decade were Asian: China, Thailand, South Korea, Indonesia, and Taiwan. Certainly Vietnam will soon be added to this list.

The increasing role of the central banks of these countries in international monetary matters and the disastrous experiences that they have had with their dollar holdings in the past will also play a role in the global process of shifting from the dollar to the yen for reserve purposes. As has already been noted, these countries all find themselves in a bind due to the fact that their income from trade is in dollars while their borrowings are increasingly in yen. As trade follows investment—with Japan being the world's largest creditor nation—it is clear that Japanese trade with all of these countries will increase rapidly in the years to come. It will thus be in the interest of all concerned in Asia to gradually shift from the dollar to the yen, both for billing and for reserve purposes. The fact that Japan, like Germany, has consistently had one of the lowest rates of inflation in the developed world will only add to the yen's attractiveness.

As Robert S. Hsu points out in his book *The MIT Encyclopedia of the Japanese Economy,* the role of the yen previously in international trade and finance has been relatively small. In 1991, it was used in only 39.4 percent of Japan's exports and 15.6 percent of its imports; ten years earlier only 29.6 percent of exports and just 2.4 percent of imports were in yen. There was also a big jump in the yen's share of the official holdings of foreign exchange. In 1990 it was 9.1 percent, compared to just 4.4 percent in 1980, when the dollar's share was still at 68.6 percent and the deutsche mark at only 14.9 percent.

One reason for this, Hsu points out, is that in order for foreigners to hold financial instruments denominated in yen for liquidity and investment and to pay for imports, the access to such instruments must be relatively free from controls. This, he points out, is not the case. Japan lacks well-developed short-term financial markets that would satisfy foreigners' needs for liquid and safe financial instruments. Its treasury bill and commercial paper markets are not well developed; restrictions even exist on some Euro-yen investments. These factors reduce the yen's ability to serve as a medium of exchange in international financial markets and as a reserve currency for official holdings of foreign exchange.

Another reason for the current restricted use of the yen in international transactions is that the bankers' acceptance market in

Japan is not well developed, which makes it difficult for Japanese firms to obtain trade financing in yen. This also explains why Japanese banks borrow overseas in foreign currencies to make foreign currency loans to domestic firms, so-called impact loans—to take advantage of the less stringent regulation of such loans.

When all these reasons are looked at together, one could expect that the yen share of total central banks' reserves would rise in the future, but not in any spectacular way—about 15 percent of total currency reserves by the end of the decade. The dollar's role as a reserve currency is bound to diminish for the same reasons that the roles of the deutsche mark and the yen are bound to increase. But is the dollar in the process of going the way of the pound sterling after World War II—sinking into irrelevance as a world currency? Paul Krugman discusses this possibility in his book *Currencies and Crisises* and does not dismiss it out of hand should a worst-case scenario for the dollar actually come to pass. As he puts it:

> The use of a currency as an international money itself reinforces that currency's usefulness, so there is an element of circular causation. It is this circularity that raises the most worries about the future prospects of the dollar. The troublesome possibilities are either that the dollar's fundamental advantage will drop to some critical point, leading to an abrupt unraveling of its international role, or that a temporary disruption of world financial markets will permanently impair the dollar's usefulness. These are not purely academic speculations, since they have precedent in the history of sterling's decline. The disruption of World War I led to a permanent reduction in sterling's role, while the gradual relative decline of Britain's importance in the world was reflected not in a smooth decline in sterling's role but in surprising persistence followed by abrupt collapse.[3]

Barring some major disruption in the system (Krugman uses the example of a war scare in Europe that could lead to capital flight and the imposition of exchange controls, which, if they lasted long enough, could break the world's habit of doing business in dollars), it will be the relative share of the United States of world output and trade that will ultimately determine the fate of the dollar as a reserve currency. Although that share continues to decline very gradually, it has hardly come close to reaching some critical point, nor will it in the immediate future. While the United States is currently experiencing a major economic revival, its two "rivals"—Japan and Germany—are either still stuck in recession, as is the case of Germany, or faced with limited growth prospects, as is the case with Japan. There is, then, no parallel between the relative position of the United States of today in the world economy and that of post–World War II Britain. In the end, the dollar will continue to be the world's chief reserve currency, with its share of total central bank currency reserves remaining above 50 percent in the foreseeable future.

11

SO HOW DIFFERENT WILL THE WORLD ECONOMY BE following the currency crisis of 1995? What lessons has the world to learn from it, and what should its leaders do to prevent even more serious crises from arising in the future?

We started this book by describing what triggered the crisis in the first place—the collapse of the Mexican peso. It was the American-sponsored $52 billion bailout that prevented that situation from turning into a full-blown global financial crisis. So it seems logical that here is where prophylactic measures are most urgently required.

The G-7 meeting in Halifax, Canada, in mid-June 1995 came up with a plan to address this issue. The world's seven most powerful nations agreed to double the amount of funds that will be available to the International Monetary Fund for use within the framework of the General Arrangements to Borrow. Although the IMF will rely chiefly upon the G-7 members to provide it with the $56 billion in emergency funding to bail out the Mexicos of the future, it now intends to ask other relatively rich nonmembers such as Austria, Spain, Australia, and especially the successful Asian nations to join the general agreement. The IMF will also set up an "early warning system" that allows it to move in before a full-fledged crisis breaks out. In order for this to work, the IMF will need accurate information, so the G-7 called for increasing transparency where critical financial data is concerned, such as the *true* amount of a country's currency reserves and the short-term claims on it.

All this is certainly a big improvement. But the G-7 did nothing to rein in the hedge funds and other financial institutions that were behind the currency speculation that fueled the yen/dollar crisis that followed the peso crisis. The markets—and the immense vested interests behind them who want to maintain the status quo—have simply outgrown governments' ability to regulate them. Over the last decade, bond issues have tripled, securities transactions have increased more than tenfold, and foreign exchange transactions have quadrupled to $1 trillion, according to the IMF. The prime minister of Canada, Jean Chrétien, summed up the collective resignation of the G-7 leaders on this issue: "We cannot simply expect those famous currency speculators to shut off their computer terminals, hang up their red suspenders, and get a life."[1]

In trade matters, the G-7 leaders demonstrated a pointed lack of endorsement of the unilateral action that the United States had taken against Japan in its "car trade war." In fact, it expressly stated that such disputes should be arbitrated within the framework of the new World Trade Organization. However, it would be a mistake to simply cast the total blame on the Clinton administration for adopting mistaken tactics. The intransigence of the Japanese government on this issue must share a good part of the fault. Put simply, Japan failed to grasp how deep sentiments run on this issue in the United States. The American public has been told time and time again that every billion dollars of new American exports result in the creation of approximately 20,000 new American jobs. Six billion dollars more car parts exported to Japan translates into 120,000 American jobs. Since this must also be true for Japan, its huge car exports to the United States must create a huge number of jobs in Japan. So, the American public concludes, why can't the Japanese give a little of that back without our having to hassle them? In some cars that they build in the United States, over 70 percent of the parts are American made and no one can see any difference in the quality of these cars as compared with those built entirely of Japanese components in Japan. So quality is an excuse, not a reason. In the minds of most Americans—who

know nothing about "managed trade" versus free trade, and who think that David Ricardo is probably a guy who plays second base for the New York Yankees—the issue reduces itself to a pure and simple matter of fairness.

This bitter issue that arose between the United States and Japan will fortunately not affect the basic alliance between these two nations. There is simply too much that ties them together, too much responsibility that both nations must jointly bear if the post–Cold War era is going to remain one of relative peace and rising prosperity.

We are moving from one major historical epoch to another. The rearrangement of the global balance of power that is now in irreversible motion will be similar in magnitude and importance to that which emerged at the end of the Napoleonic Wars, the framework for which was established in 1815 at the Council of Vienna and endured for the century that followed.

The hallmark of that first epoch in modern history was the strategic balance of power among the key European powers: Britain, France, Prussia/Germany, the Austro-Hungarian empire, and Czarist Russia. The United States stood apart in splendid isolation, as did Japan, with the exception of its brief clash with Russia in 1905. This "order" fell apart with the beginning of World War I in 1914. In contrast to the Council of Vienna, the Treaty of Versailles, which signalled the end of that first major conflict of the twentieth century, did nothing to establish a new world order. An uneasy interregnum typified the two decades that followed and ended with the outbreak of World War II in 1939.

The end of that war in 1945 resulted in the de facto establishment of a new world order. The Western European powers were now but shadows of their former selves, and Japan's brief adventure on the world scene had ended badly. The new era was now one of global domination by the two victorious superpowers, a bipolar world in which the United States and the Soviet Union stood in near-deadly confrontation for the next 44 years. It was the era of cold war, one that always carried with it the threat of a global nuclear holocaust. Containment of the

Soviet Union and the avoidance of such a war completely overshadowed all other items on the American national agenda.

Now that it is clear that the bipolar world of 1945-1991 is a thing of the past, the key questions facing us today are: What is going to replace it? What roles will the United States, Japan, and the European Union play in this New World Order? To begin with, it will be primarily economic, not military, strength that will determine the new global pecking order. In addition, the key players in this New World Order will no longer be nation states standing alone but rather key nation states as leaders of regional economic groupings. Of these, three nations and their groupings will *initially* be vying for leadership status in the world of the 1990s and beyond. This triad consists of:

- Germany and the European Union with their new economic "satellites" in Eastern Europe. In currency terms, this is the deutsche mark/Euro bloc.
- Japan and its "zone of influence" stretching from Singapore to Hong Kong to Taiwan to South Korea. This is the yen bloc.
- The United States, its partners in the North American Free Trade Area, Canada and Mexico, and their "colonies" to the south in Central and South America, soon to become partners in a Western Hemisphere Common Market. This is the dollar bloc.

Although Russia, and the new confederation and common market that it will anchor, will be a candidate eventually, it will undoubtedly take at least two decades before the ruble bloc can become a major player in the world economy. This skepticism arises from the continuing failure of Russia to provide the fiscal, monetary, and legal framework necessary for the establishment of a broadly accepted free enterprise system and the prosperity it will eventually bring with it. Even when this is achieved, its scope will be limited. Russia's former Eastern Europe satellites, which had been important members of the former ruble bloc, are gone forever. The sooner all of them—led by the Czech Republic, Hungary, Poland, and the Baltic states—can formally join the EU and its currency zone, the better off they will be.

There can be little doubt that China is next in line to ascend to the top echelon of nations in terms of economic clout. The World Bank's estimate that by the year 2005 China will have the largest economy on earth is now generally accepted. Its GDP continues to grow at or near double-digit annual rates. (To be sure, the sheer size of the Chinese population and work force play a key role in this.) In per capita GDP terms, however, China will still lag far behind Japan and the West well into the twenty-first century. On the other hand, because of its uniquely large labor force, China also has the ability to combine state-of-the-art technology imported from abroad with an unlimited domestic work force that receives one of the world's lowest wages. This will allow it to very soon become a huge player in export markets around the world and, in turn, will allow it to be able to absorb immense quantities of imported goods.

But this still lies decades in the future for China. In the here and now it is the triad of the United States, Japan, and Germany that are the principal global powers. And they will stay that way well into the next century.

There can be no doubt that of the three groupings, the Pacific Rim, led by Japan, will be the most dynamic. The Asian perimeter of the Pacific, which contains only 15 percent of its land area and only one-third of its population, contributes 85 percent of its output and is already first in the world in terms of the output of steel, automobiles, and consumer electronics. As a result, the Asian side of the Pacific Rim now controls 22 percent of world GNP. The reasons why its share of world output is bound to grow are numerous: its high rates of savings and investments, the diligence of its work force, the excellence of its education system, and the fact that it takes a five-year view rather than five months or five weeks. Suffice it to say that by the year 2000, according to a team of experts at Stanford, its share of world GNP is expected to rise to 28 percent. By 2050, as the

Asian heartland is drawn into its orbit, the other side of the Pacific will probably produce 50 percent of the world's GNP.

All that can only happen, however, if Asia has free access to world markets. Western Europe does not offer such access since it is openly discriminatory against Asian-produced goods. The United States does offer such access; many Americans would say too much. On the other hand, many Japanese might say that they have been giving us too much money. Americans "expected" them, for instance, to regularly buy new issues of U.S. government notes and bonds in order to help finance the United States' huge budgetary deficits, which Americans could not finance themselves due to their low savings rate. Yet these were deficits that greatly contributed to the maintenance of economic growth in the United States since the beginning of the Reagan administration. Those deficits and that need for Japanese capital will gradually disappear. But that does not detract from the benefits that America has derived from inputs of Japanese capital in the past.

The American market will remain as much open to imports from Asia and other countries in the future as it has in the past. The Clinton administration's foray into unilateral trade warfare is strictly an aberration. It is, after all, the United States that has been the main force behind the establishment of all the supranational financial institutions where, by definition, problems are solved on a multilateral basis, including the IMF, the World Bank, the General Agreement on Tariffs and Trade, and GATT's successor, the World Trade Organization. America is committed to free trade and the freedom of international capital movements like no other country on earth. The future openness of the American markets for goods, services, and capital can be taken as a given.

To be sure, an open but stagnant market would not contribute that much to future global prosperity. But, as we have seen, the American economy is anything but stagnant. It is on a trend line of robust, sustainable growth. Schumpeter is still alive

and well in America.

Europe is another question. Its growth prospects are not that good, nor are its trade policies that open. This is why TAFTA is such a bad idea, and why a Trans-Pacific Free Trade Area is such a good idea.

Finally, friction within the triad will certainly arise if there are future currency crises of a severity equal to or even greater than the currency crisis of 1995. The key to avoiding these crises lies in convergence, a concept that lies at the very heart of the Maastricht Treaty. All three members of the triad, the United States, Japan, and Germany, are committed to achieving such convergence in rates of inflation, rates of interest, GDP/debt ratio, and the GDP/deficit ratio. Since exchange rate stability flows out of the others, it is only a matter of time before the dollar/yen/mark relationship moves into temporary equilibrium.

Epilogue

BY THE SUMMER OF 1996, that new equilibrium appears to be almost at hand. The Japanese economy has come back more quickly than many had expected. The German economy is in the process of bottoming out and seems poised for new growth. In the United States, economic growth continues to exceed most expectations, although signs of an eventual slowdown in 1997 are mounting.

Inflation and interest rate trends reenforce this view. In all three countries, the rate of inflation is very low by historical standards, and holding steady. The central banks of both Japan and Germany, after allowing domestic interest rates to fall to near-record lows in the first half of 1996, have kept them there, thus decreasing the attractiveness of both the yen and the mark for international investors. In the United States, the Federal Reserve, after lowering short-term rates three times between July of 1995 and March of 1996, has decided against any further monetary easing, while long-term interest rates, after bottoming out at the end of 1995, continue to rise, making the dollar, on balance, increasingly attractive to international investors.

These trends reflect a major adjustment in attitude by the policymakers in all three of the countries that control the world's monetary system. Germany's central bank, the Bundesbank, facing 11 percent unemployment and rising labor unrest, has finally relented in its policy of promoting an ultra-strong DM no matter what the cost in terms of economic growth and domestic employment. Japan's central bank has also relented in its fight to curb inflation at any cost and has expanded the domestic money supply at a torrid pace so as to promote the return of economic growth. This policy has contributed to the weakening of both the yen and mark.

In the United States, just the opposite has occurred. Where the dollar is concerned, both the Treasury and the Federal Reserve have rejected earlier policies of benign neglect. Secretary of the Treasury Rubin has stated repeatedly that a strong dollar is in the interests of the United States and should not be used as a tool to reduce the U.S. trade deficit. At the end of May 1996, Mr. William McDonough, president of the Federal Reserve Bank of New York, which is responsible for the Fed's intervention in foreign exchange markets, put it even more forcefully: "I am a very, very strong believer in a strong dollar being good for the United States and the world."

All this has been reflected in the currency markets. The yen has fallen substantially, settling in at what appears to be the temporary equilibrium level of 105-110 to the dollar. The mark has also decreased in value and seems to have found its equilibrium level at 1.50-1.55 to the dollar . . . at least for the time being. Thus convergence of economic conditions within the Triad has led to the return of calm in the currency markets. The speculators have gone back into the woodwork.

Outside of the Triad, the issue of China has suddenly come to the fore. Its refusal to put a stop to the piracy of American intellectual property, ranging from CDs to computer software, led to a showdown between China and the United States, reminiscent of the situation the year before between Japan and the United States on the issue of vehicle trade. Nevertheless, the United States has agreed to extend most-favored-nation status to China in the face of its rapidly rising importance to the United States in both economic and geopolitical terms. This represents irrevocable recognition of the fact that this nation of 1.2 billion people, with one of the highest economic growth rates in the world, is destined to become a superpower in every sense early in the twenty-first century. There are many who see the eventual return to a bipolar world as a result. Just as the American market was key to the resurgence of both Europe and Japan after World War II, so today American trade is of critical importance to the rise of China. To put it in perspective, the value of China-U.S. trade is equal to 8.3 percent of China's GDP, while representing only 0.8 percent of American GDP. The United States government will continue to encourage the growth of the China trade as the most important component of a policy aimed at bringing China into the family of nations through "engagement."

This is giving rise to new problems, however, for just as trade with Japan seems to be coming into balance, a huge and growing trade deficit is developing with China. From the American perspective, it seems that just when we begin to gain ground in one place, we lose it in another. This increases the likelihood that we will have no choice but to export $150 billion, year after year, to cover our continuing huge trade deficits. This would mean that the amount of dollars and government bonds and notes in foreign hands will increase with each passing year, rising inexorably toward the two trillion mark. That would be tantamount to the creation of a "dollar bubble" of unprecedented size, which, in turn, could be the precursor of the Currency Crisis of '97 or '99.

Such an outlook leads me to these conclusions: The Tug of War will continue. New currency crises will inevitably arise. During them, each country will once again scramble to protect its own national interests. There will be winners and losers. But I have no doubt that the United States will remain the world's dominant power, and the dollar the world's dominant currency.

NOTES

Chapter 4

1. Martin Feldstein. "Stabilize the Prices, Not the Dollar," *The Wall Street Journal*, March 17, 1995.
2. Quoted in Paul Krugman, *Currencies and Crises* (Cambridge: MIT Press, 1995), p. 13.
3. Paul McCracken, "Falling Dollar? Blame the Deficit," *The Wall Street Journal*, April 13, 1995.

Chapter 5

1. Mark A. Miles and Richard M. Salsman, "Why is the Dollar Falling? It Isn't," *The Wall Street Journal*, April 6, 1995, p. A16.
2. David E. Sanger, "Car Wars: The Corrosion at the Core of Pax Pacifica," *The New York Times*, May 14, 1995, sec. 4, p. 1.

Chapter 6

1. C. Fred Bergsten, "Aluminum Tests Clinton's Mettle," *The Wall Street Journal*, January 1, 1994, p.A10.
2. Martin Feldstein, "Lower Deficits, Lower Dollar," *The Wall Street Journal*, May 16, 1995, p. A18.
3. Paul Krugman, *Currencies and Crises* (Cambridge: MIT Press, 1995), p. 25.
4. Paul Krugman, "Why Higher Savings Might Hit the Dollar," *The Financial Times*, May 24, 1995. Here, and throughout, emphasis within quotations has been added by the author.

Chapter 7

1. Paul Krugman, *Currencies and Crises* (Cambridge: MIT Press, 1995), p. 167-168.

2. Quoted in Paul Craig Roberts, "The inevitable decline of a reserve currency," *The Wall Street Journal*, March 16, 1995, p. A22.

3. Quoted in "Heard on the Street," *The Wall Street Journal*, March 1, 1993.

4. Krugman, *Currencies and Crises*, p. 35 (emphasis added).

5. *The Economist*, November 18, 1995, p. 18.

Chapter 8

1. Benjamin M. Friedman, *Day of Reckoning: The Consequences of Economic Policy in the 1980s* (New York: Random House, 1988), p. 8.

2. Judy Shelton, *Money Meltdown: Restoring Order to the Global Currency System* (New York: The Free Press, 1994).

3. Christopher Wood, *The End of Japan, Inc.* (New York: Simon and Schuster, 1994).

4. Thomas F. McClarty, III, "Hemispheric Free Trade Is Still a National Priority," *The Wall Street Journal*, May 26, 1995, p. A11.

5. James Meade, *Problems of Economic Union*, p. 8.

6. "Technology versus Tulips," *The Financial Times* (emphasis added).

Chapter 9

1. "Now Hear This," *The Wall Street Journal*.

2. "Japan, Eek," *The Wall Street Journal*, June 1, 1995, p. A15.

3. Christopher Wood, *The End of Japan, Inc.* (New York: Simon and Schuster, 1994), p. 67.

4. Ibid., p. 68.

5. Bob Barbera, *Capital Investments International*, March 27, 1995.

6. Philip Gawith, "From Strength to Strength," *The Financial Times*, June 6, 1995.

7. Ibid.

8. James Fallows, NPR Commentary, March 15, 1995.

9. Wood, *The End of Japan, Inc.*, p. 223.

Chapter 10

1. "Brussels launches single currency campaign," *The Financial Times,* May 31, 1995.
2. Quoted in Ian Black, "Rifkind talks tough on EU," *Guardian,* September 22, 1995, p. 1.
3. Paul Krugman, *Currencies and Crises* (Cambridge: MIT Press, 1995), p. 179.

Chapter 11

1. Quoted in Clyde Farnsworth, "Bagpipes and Bailouts as Leaders Meet," *New York Times,* June 15, 1995.

INDEX

Entries in italics refer to tables and figures.